T

SURREY

Village Book

THE VILLAGES OF BRITAIN SERIES

Other counties in the series include:

Bedfordshire	Lincolnshire
Berkshire	Norfolk
Buckinghamshire	Northumberland
Cheshire	Northamptonshire
Cleveland	Nottinghamshire
Cornwall	Oxfordshire
Cumbria	Powys Montgomeryshire
Derbshire	Shropshire
Devon	Somerset
Dorset	Staffordshire
Durham	Suffolk
Essex	Surrey
Glamorgan	East Sussex
Gloucestershire	West Sussex
Gwent	Warwickshire
Hampshire	West Midlands
Herefordshire	Wiltshire
Hertfordshire	Worcestershire
Kent	East Yorkshire
Lancashire	North Yorkshire
Leicestershire & Rutland	South & West Yorkshire

A list of the volumes currently available can be obtained
by writing to the publisher.

The
SURREY
Village Book
GRAHAM COLLYER

with illustrations by Christopher Howkins

COUNTRYSIDE BOOKS
NEWBURY, BERKSHIRE

First published 1984
New edition 1998
©Graham Collyer 1984, 1998

COUNTRYSIDE BOOKS
3 Catherine Road
Newbury, Berkshire

ISBN 1 85306 549 8

Designed by Graham Whiteman

Map by Trevor Yorke

Front cover photo of Chiddingfold and back cover photo of
Wonersh, both supplied by Andy Williams

Produced through MRM Associates Ltd., Reading

Printed in Great Britain by
J. W. Arrowsmith Ltd., Bristol

To Ann, David, Laurie and Esther

N

EGHAM

STAINES

Virginia Water

Lyne

Chertsey

Wall on Tha

WEYBRIDGE

Bagshot

Lightwater

Chobham

Byfleet

Cobh

Bisley

WOKING

Pyrford

Stok d'Aberr

Alford

CAMBERLEY

Brookwood

Send

Ockham

FRIMLEY

Pirbright

Worplesdon

West Horsley

West Clandon

East Horsle

Ash

GUILDFORD

Gomsha

Puttenham

Shalford

Shere

Abing

FARNHAM

Seale

Bramley

Holmbu St Ma

Tilford

Elstead

GODALMING

Milford

Shamley Green

Ewh

Millbridge

Busbridge

Thursley

Hascombe

CRANLEIGH

Churt

Hindhead

Grayswood

Alfold

Shottermill

Chiddingfold

HAZLEMERE

HER

ott

EPSOM

BANSTEAD

Newark Priory, Send.

Ashtead

Chipstead

Warlingham

rcham

Woldingham

am LEATHERHEAD

Kingswood

Caterham

LIMPSFIELD

gham

Oxted

Betchworth

Godstone

REIGATE

Blechingley

Brockham

REDHILL

DORKING

tcott

Salfords

Crowhurst

Holmwood

Outwood

HORLEY

Smallfield

LINGFIELD

Dormansland

st

Newdigate

Charlwood

Capel

ley

County of
Surrey

🍁 INTRODUCTION

It was William Cobbett who wrote in October 1825: 'Those that travel on turnpike roads know nothing of England.' Cobbett was a Surrey man, born in a farmhouse in Farnham. I, too, am a Surrey man, born in a wartime nursing home in Rowledge, no more than three miles from Cobbett's birthplace. My family's roots are deep in the sandy soil of South West Surrey; the spelling of my surname is the Surrey form.

My years as a junior reporter on the *Farnham Herald* took me to every village and hamlet in South West Surrey. I was encouraged to get to know the places and the people by my news editor, the late Mr L.T. Pope, who was, I think, the greatest influence on my chosen career. He also fostered my great love of village cricket and this is reflected in many of the passages on the pages which follow.

Now, as editor of the *Surrey Advertiser*, I am based in the county town of Guildford and surrounded by villages, some still quite rural, many with a more modern appearance and home to people who earn their living in the capital. Cobbett would, I suppose, be shocked if he could see Surrey in the twilight of the 20th century. His *Rural Rides* can be, and indeed have been, retraced, but so much of what the great man saw has disappeared. Those who love the county must be on their guard to protect their heritage from over-zealous planners and despoilers of the countryside.

Since the first *Surrey Village Book* was published in 1984, much has changed, and not always for the better. But as we approach the Millennium, there are groups and individuals across the county who are endeavouring to leave a legacy of good architecture and planning for future generations.

Cobbett's turnpikes may have been replaced by fast trunk roads and even faster motorways, both of which criss-cross

Surrey, but away from these are the lanes and the byways along which the best of any county can be seen. Surrey's network of lanes, with their high hedgerows and secluded cottages, are a delight. I did not know how much I loved the county until I returned to it after six years abroad, and that was when I set out to discover more.

I hope in this book to show how enjoyable such journeys of discovery can be.

Graham Collyer
Hindhead
1998

❧ ABINGER

Lutyens was at work in Abinger to the south of the A25. He built Goddards in 1898-9 as a hostel for young women and then added two rooms a decade later when the property was converted to a private house. The great Surrey architect also converted a 17th century cottage into a post office in 1899 but this is once more a cottage.

There is a war memorial by Lutyens in the churchyard of St James's which is claimed to be the second highest old parish church in the county, the church at Coldharbour being the highest. It was bombed during the war, restored in 1950 and then again 14 years later after a fire. When the German flying bomb struck in 1944, it destroyed the organ, and at the beginning of the last decade of the century it was decided to replace the 'temporary' electronic instrument that had supplied the church music for more than 50 years with a new organ for the Millennium, to be built specially for St James's and similar to the one that Jerry took out.

Near the church, and almost lost in the passing years, is St James's Well which was built by William John Evelyn, Lord of the Manor of Abinger, and declared open to the parishioners on 11 August 1893. The now demolished Abinger Hall was where Darwin used Roman mosaic floors in a field to observe the earthworm.

The hamlet of Sutton to the west has two old farmhouses; one, Sutton Place Farm, which was built around 1700, the other, Fulvens, which is earlier and stated by Pevsner and Nairn to be one of the best farms in the county. The residents of Sutton have been plagued by lorries in the narrow lanes, caused it seems by the much larger Sutton, once of the county but now in Greater London, continuing to have Surrey as part of its address. This hamlet is a far cry from any London borough.

🍁 ABINGER HAMMER

Everyone who travels the A25 through Abinger Hammer knows of the village clock. It stands proudly over the winding street and on the hour Jack the Hammer strikes out the time on his anvil. The clock, given in memory of the first Lord Farrer of Abinger Hall who died in 1899, reminds us of the importance of this area in the Surrey iron industry of long ago. The Tillingbourne stream was dammed at various points to create the hammer ponds the iron masters required to carry out their craft, and these have now been utilised by watercress growers who find the chalk beds ideal for their product. The first modern watercress beds in Britain were started in 1808, and those at Abinger Hammer were formed 42 years later.

Abinger Hammer is a popular spot in summer but the narrowness of the main road is a source of irritation. Cricket is played beside the road on land given as a memorial to the men from the village who died in the Great War. North of the A25 Hackhurst Downs rise to 733ft and there is a granite pillar marking the spot where Samuel Wilberforce, who was Bishop of Winchester and son of the abolitionist William Wilberforce, was thrown from his horse and fatally injured in 1873.

The people of Abinger Hammer run their own village school, recognised by the Charity Commissioners after the county council withdrew its support in 1982. The school is on a rise behind the famous clock and first opened for business in 1873, the gift of Thomas Henry Farrer and his wife. Five years later Farrer handed over the reins to a local committee, and alterations followed in 1881 and 1893 before the county took control in 1906. Fortunately, the county did not become the owner of the building and this proved to be vital when the decision came from the education committee to close the school.

🍁 ALBURY

Magisterial orders in 1784 began a process that was not completed until well into the 19th century. The result was that the present village of Albury was established, with the great architect Pugin influencing the style. His delightful chimneys are still in evidence today. The village was formerly in Albury Park and the move was completed when the estate was bought by Henry Drummond, an MP and wealthy banker, in 1819. In 1840 Drummond built the Catholic Apostolic church for the Irvingite Sect and it stands as a striking landmark near the junction of the A25 and the A248 into the village.

Close to that junction is the Silent Pool, more properly Shireborne Pond, a popular spot with walkers which has become a victim of climate change, although some argue that the dearth of water is due more to the changes in abstraction policy by the local water authority. The pool in another age was a wonderfully calm oasis of reflections, kingfishers and fish swimming lazily. Legend has it that in the 12th century King John discovered Emma, a woodcutter's daughter, swimming naked there. The girl took fright and drowned, taking her brother, who had tried to rescue her, with her. The ghost of Emma is said to haunt the pool which, sadly, is not the place it was. The Silent Pool was the location for Martin Tupper's fictitious novel, *Stephan Langton*. Tupper, largely unknown today but a literary giant in the Victorian era, lived in Albury for 40 years, before moving to South London where he died in 1889. He was buried in the parish churchyard, despite the claim on a vault at the original parish church in Albury Park.

Cobbett and, earlier, John Evelyn the diarist concerned themselves with Albury. Cobbett, on one of his rides, indulged in what he called a 'pretty bare-faced' move by entering Albury Park and asking for Mr Drummond's permission to continue on through in order to reach Shere. The request was not only granted, said Cobbett, but the 'prettiest' gardens in England were opened up for his perusal. Evelyn was credited with making the gardens.

A mill and a church in Albury were recorded in the Domesday survey, but there have been several mills in the district, one of which was burned down on 13 November 1830. According to the *Surrey Advertiser*, in a historical note, one 'Doggy' Warner was the culprit. He also shot at the miller, James Franks, and after a trial at Guildford Assizes went to the gallows. Almost 250 years earlier there was another hanging being talked about in the village although as was the custom in Elizabethan times the punishment did not fit the crime.

Robert Wintershull, gent., of Albury, was hanged for burglary. He was found guilty of entering the house of a fellow villager, William Otway, and stealing a coverlet and three pillowbars valued at £3.

🍁 ALFOLD

There are so many pretty approaches to Surrey's parish churches but the path up to St Nicholas's at Alfold surely cannot be bettered for simplicity and beauty. Everything is in scale as one looks towards the church from the village square. Old cottages on the right look out on to the stocks and across the fields to Sussex. The cobbled path takes the visitor to the churchyard gate and beyond to the little church, which dates from 1100. The Great Storm of 1987 caused severe damage to the church which English Heritage has described as 'an ancient building of high worth'. The yew in the churchyard is as old as any in the county, and it was Eric Parker who noticed that it stands 'almost in a mathematically straight line' with the yews at Dunsfold and Hambledon.

Alfold, which has the Sussex border at its doorstep, had no made-up roads until 1809 and was as rural a place as one could find. And yet more than 200 years before that it was a bustling glass-making centre. A slab of Sussex marble in the churchyard is said to mark the grave of Jean Carre who was one of the last French glass-makers in the Fold country. The industry was carried out in Sidney Wood and Carré had been granted a licence five years before his death in 1572 to make glass similar to that in his own country.

The village, which in days gone by was on a smuggling route from the Sussex coast, when tobacco and brandy were left at Alfold farmhouses at the dead of night, in return for food, was considered early in the 1990s as the site of a new housing initiative by the projects office overseen by the Prince of Wales, and although this idea was abandoned the future expansion of Alfold has not been ruled out.

🍁 ARTINGTON

The trees have grown so tall on St Catherine's Hill that the ruins of a chapel on its top are no longer easily discernible to the passer-by. Which is a shame because those old sandstones have been a landmark for centuries. St Catherine's Chapel dates from 1317 but was undoubtedly built on the site of a much earlier place of worship.

Folklore has it that two sisters were responsible for building the chapel, and that of St Martha a few miles away. It was said they threw a hammer back and forth to each other. The inside measurement is 45ft 6in by 20ft 6in, and it had five doors which is curious in so small a building. Two of them were let into windows so it seems likely that ladders were used to allow access to upstairs accommodation.

The ruins are close to what has become popularly known as the Pilgrims' Way, a footpath that has been used for centuries by all manner of people. The path crossed the river into Shalford meadows where there was a large annual fair in medieval times. The crossing was either by punt or plank, and it is not so long ago that a boat was used to carry pedestrians. Now there is a modern footbridge.

The old coaching route to Portsmouth runs below St Catherine's and the railway line enters a tunnel beneath the hill. The community of Artington has been affected by the increased traffic flow on the main road from Guildford to Godalming, but has been changed little by the presence of the headquarters of Surrey Police, in the former manor house at Mount Browne, off Sandy Lane, and the Guildford branch of the College of Law in the converted Braboeuf Manor, opposite St Catherine's Hill.

However, its open space has been in the news of late with the donation of a piece of land owned by the Loseley Estate for use as a children's hospice which will be built, some say incongruously, beside the main railway line and next to a terminal for a park and ride scheme, something that Guildford Borough Council sees as the town's saviour from death by traffic strangulation.

🍁 ASH

The parish is in the Borough of Guildford but is always associated with Aldershot because of its close proximity to the Hampshire town. The county boundary is all that separates the two. Ribbon development between Ash and Ash Vale has taken away any last vestige of village appearance. A 10-mile-long dual carriageway linking the A31 at Runfold and the M3 at Frimley takes traffic swiftly past Ash. The £140 million Blackwater Valley Road was completed in August 1996 when the three-mile centre section was opened. It was hailed as a major achievement for the engineers and road builders who had to divert the river Blackwater and construct an aqueduct to carry the Basingstoke Canal, in addition to spending almost £1 million on providing special features for animal and plant life. The road has led to new industry being established in the Blackwater Valley which has created not only jobs but increased traffic. So, while on the one hand villages like Ash and Tongham have had some relief, the feeder roads have tended to become busier as drivers discover the merits of the BVR and its links to the burgeoning Thames Valley business area and beyond.

Old Ash can still be seen between the church of St Peter and the Greyhound public house. A cottage close to the church used to be the Harts Horn Inn where, it is said, Dick Turpin was a visitor. In truth, if there is such a thing in this instance, another highwayman, Jeremiah Abershaw, could have been the robber in question for it was he who appeared at nearby Guildford Sessions on Wednesday, 8 August 1792. Abershaw, a 22-year-old shoemaker, had been accused the previous day of felonious assault on the King's Highway in the County of Essex. He was charged with stealing a gold watch and other things. Abershaw, whose real name was said to be Avershaw, was tried at Croydon on 30 July 1795, and hanged on Kennington Common.

🍁 ASHFORD

Ashford Common, where cavalry regiments were reviewed by the King in the early 1800s, was probably the traditional meeting place of the Spelthorne Hundred when the area was in Middlesex. Now there is very little open space left in Spelthorne, the borough that was created in 1974 and which added a sizeable northern area to Surrey.

Spelthorne is administered from Staines and overflown in no uncertain manner by the jets which use London Airport at Heathrow. Much of its area is covered by water for it is a borough of reservoirs, some purpose built, others formed from old gravel workings.

Ashford, which was known as Exeford in Domesday times, has always been associated with Staines and became part of an urban district in 1930. St Matthew's church was built about 1860 and part of the cost was defrayed by the Welsh School which came to the village at the time the church was being constructed. Now St David's Girls School it received – in exchange for its help – 212 seats in perpetuity. In the churchyard is a floor slab which marks the site of a Norman chancel.

❧ ASH GREEN

The approach along White Lane from the Hog's Back is still quite rural, and it is not until the main road is reached, adjacent to Ash station on the Reading to Tonbridge railway line, that there is a sense of the large, sprawling parish being heavily developed. There was a station at Ash Green itself until the 1960s. The once popular Farnham to Guildford line carried passengers to the county town without the need for a change of trains at Aldershot. The station was built in 1851, and film buffs will recall that it was used for the 1937 Will Hay classic *Oh, Mr Porter*. It has now been converted to a private residence, and the line, where access continues to be possible, is used by walkers and riders.

One of the oldest properties in Ash Green is the listed Ashe Grange in Foreman Road, which was built in 1820 for the Staffordshire pottery giant William Spode, when he retired to the village. Derelict for years, it is now a home for the elderly.

❧ ASHTEAD

Samuel Pepys wrote about Ashtead in his diaries, about the 'little hole' he could not stand upright in where he stayed overnight. On 25 July 1663, he wrote: 'When we come there (Epsom) we could hear of no lodging, the town so full; but, which was better, I went towards Ashtead, my old place of pleasure, and there by direction of one goodman Arthur, whom we met on the way, we went to Farmer Page's, at which direction he and I made good sport, and there we got a lodging in a little hole we could not stand upright in, but rather than go further to look we staid there, and while supper was getting ready I took him to walk up and down behind my cozen Pepys' house that was, which I find comes little short of what I took it to be when I was a little boy.' The year before Pepys had written: 'I eat, among other fruit, much mulberrys, a thing I have not eat of these many years, since I used to be at Ashtead, at my cozen Pepys.'

Ashtead is on the main road between Leatherhead and Epsom. Ashtead woods and common are beloved of walkers and riders and Ashtead Park has some open space. A Romano-British villa was found on the common in 1926 and contained 12 rooms and a four-room bath annexe. There was a large bath house some distance away, and some of the tiles which were decorated with hunting scenes were incorporated in the church of St Giles. The villa was occupied between the first and third centuries as revealed by coins and pottery found at the site.

🍁 ASH VALE

The northern end of the parish of Ash is heavily built up but close to common land and the lakes through which the county boundary runs alongside the Blackwater Valley Road. Ash Vale station is on the Waterloo line and was opened on 2 May 1870. Queen Victoria was once brought to the station by train en route to review the troops at Aldershot.

A grisly moment in the history of the station occurred in August 1952 when a booking clerk was murdered. A former guardsman was convicted of the murder in November that year and sentenced to death.

🍁 BADSHOT LEA

In spite of the close proximity of both Farnham and Aldershot, Badshot Lea has survived to retain its own identity. Old kilns and oast houses are a reminder of the hop fields which once covered the land in this part of the county. Badshot Lea is a village that is interested in its history, and one recent exhibition explained the legend of the Badshot Lea 'docks' which has fascinated people for decades. How could a small village, situated miles from the sea, have a docks? The answer, apparently, was to be found in the terrible flooding the village endured in times gone by. The road near the Aldershot boundary became a pond and, at the turn of the century, the area was nicknamed the 'docks'.

For 34 years William Rankine was the headmaster of the village school. A Scot who came to Farnham with his parents, he became a leading authority on the Mesolithic period. His archaeological work in the district had always been much valued, but it was not until 1983 that his discoveries were seen by the public when an exhibition was mounted in Farnham Museum. Until then the artefacts had lain in cardboard boxes gathering dust since the former teacher's death in 1962.

🍁 BAGSHOT

Bagshot Heath was 'not only good for little but good for nothing', said Defoe. The heath was the haunt of highwaymen and other undesirables, but it was the source of fuel. Turf sold for 2s 6d a load. However, improved husbandry in the 18th century brought about a change. In 1754 the Rev Edward Cooper said he thought the soil was too poor to bear wheat, but then someone introduced chalk – brought by wagon from the Hog's Back at Seale – and clover seeds, and the condition of the soil was enhanced.

Extensive nurseries were established and today Bagshot is famous for its rhododendrons and azaleas. Eric Parker said: 'To imagine Bagshot without rhododendrons is to think of

Mitcham without lavender, Epsom without salts, Farnham without hops.' Gardeners come from far and wide to buy from the nurseries alongside the A30 which in recent years has given up much of its through traffic to the M3.

Bagshot became an important staging post in the days of the coach and four, and in busy times as many as 30 changes of horses were made in the village. There were 14 inns to cater for the visitors. The Jolly Farmer, it is said, used to be known as the Golden Farmer because of a notorious highwayman on the heath who touched nothing but gold and a farmer at nearby Frimley who paid his debts only in gold. The two were at last recognised as the same person, and the inn is close to the spot where the villain was hanged.

St Anne's church has memorials to members of the Royal Family given by the Duke of Connaught who lived at Bagshot Park.

🍁 BAYNARDS

The old station and the Thurlow Arms at Baynards give the appearance of being caught in a time warp. When Dr Beeching brought his axe down on the Guildford to Horsham railway line in 1965 it signalled the end of the working life of Baynards station which had served the big house, Baynards Park, and the local brick-making industry. Now, it is both a private residence and a rail enthusiast's dream. It is as if time has stood still. Metal advertisement signs continue to promote Colman's Mustard, Colman's Starch and Nestles Milk. Listen carefully and you can convince yourself that you can hear the approach of the 10.50 from Guildford via Cranleigh which will stop at Baynards before entering West Sussex and a tunnel as it departs for Horsham.

Baynards Park was built by Sir George More of Loseley in the late 16th century and was rebuilt after being destroyed by fire.

The Downs Link path which joins the North and South Downs in places utilises the bed of the old railway line. It is 32 miles long with a 4-mile extension towards the coast, and its northerly starting point is at St Martha's church, high above Chilworth.

🍁 BEACON HILL

North of the A3 and the traffic-affected crossroads at Hindhead, Beacon Hill has its own identity and is where the majority of Hindhead residents live. Once a remote, self-contained hilltop village, it is now home to commuters both to London and neighbouring towns. Time was when Beacon Hill residents wanted for nothing, so varied and numerous were the shops and trades that were on hand, but although businesses are fewer in number now they nevertheless continue to provide a valuable service.

The village school, built in 1906, fought off possible closure by meeting the county council's age of transfer changes head on in the early 1990s and transforming itself into a vibrant junior establishment which is very much the centre of the community. Children at the school continue to benefit from the generosity of Sir Alfred Yarrow, a great shipbuilder and founder of the eponymous shipyard on the Clyde, who lived in Beacon Hill for many years before his death in 1932. He established the Yarrow Educational Trust in 1917 and later built at his own expense the village club which subsequently became the Royal British Legion club.

Sir Alfred, a teetotaller, would not allow alcohol to be consumed in the village club, and it was some years after he died that the British Legion moved from its limited accommodation at the Woodcock public house to the spaciousness of the by now non-dry premises.

Just like their Victorian and Edwardian predecessors, Beacon Hill residents have thousands of acres of open space on their doorstep. Much of it is owned by the National Trust, including the Golden Valley which was bought at auction in Guildford in 1928 by the birth control pioneer Marie Stopes when it was feared that it might fall into the hands of property developers. Miss Stopes, who lived in Tower Road on the edge of the valley, had one motive: to save it for the nation. She sold it on to the National Trust, whose local committee raised the money by public subscription.

🍁 BETCHWORTH

Travellers by train on the picturesque line between Guildford and Redhill pass through Betchworth station but see nothing of the village, for it is to the south beyond the A25 road. It is a quiet place through which the river Mole meanders. The Domesday church has been replaced by one that retains Norman traces, and whose original tower was moved in the middle of the 19th century because it was found to be unsafe.

Among the memorials in St Michael's is one to Sir Benjamin Brodie who was a surgeon to Queen Victoria. He was one of three Betchworth doctors who cared for the Royal Family: the others being Thomas Morsted who was surgeon to Henry V and was at Agincourt, and Dyce Duckworth earlier this century.

The entrance to the churchyard is by way of a narrow path bordered by cottages opposite which is the Dolphin Inn where the landlord brewed his own ale until 1926. Across the lane which leads to Leigh are 16th century cottages said to be genuine and untouched by any fake or restoration.

There was a castle at Betchworth on a knoll above the river but it has long since gone. It was probably of 14th century origin and is likely not to have seen action. During Queen Anne's reign it fell into disrepair, was dismantled and a private house was built on the spot. But this too has disappeared.

Records show that there was a case of witchcraft in Betchworth in the 16th century, and that the defendant, George Brockham, a clerk, was tried in his absence at Southwark Assizes in March 1576 and found not guilty. His alleged crime? That he did bewitch to death a bull valued at £2! Other villagers were not so fortunate. Richard Hole, a bricklayer, appeared at Croydon Assizes in 1580 and was sentenced to hang for burglary of a house at Horley and the theft of cloth valued at £3 10s. And Michael Lamb, a yeoman, confessed to highway robbery in 1581 and 1582 and was hanged.

🍁 BISLEY

When the National Rifle Association transferred from Wimbledon to the wild common near Woking, Bisley came to the notice of the world. Now, for a fortnight in July this unlikely place plays host to top marksmen from all parts of the globe. Fame does not appear to have rubbed off on the village which goes about its daily business with barely a second thought for the crack shots out on the common.

The criminal and underworld fraternity will probably know Bisley more for Coldingley Prison, which is situated close to modern houses in the village, than for the NRA.

In days gone by the village was centred more on the ancient church of St John the Baptist, a few hundred yards from which a holy well was, by tradition, the place where children were baptised. The water in the spring was said to be colder in summer and warmer in winter.

❦ BLACKHEATH

Tucked away behind Chilworth and Wonersh, Blackheath is a delightful little place where the Villagers is a popular inn with visitors who come to enjoy the heathland walks or simply the quiet of the countryside. They come, too, to watch cricket on an attractive ground near the pub. Blackheath Cricket Club is well into its second century and its ground is among the best kept in the county. The church of St Martin was dedicated in 1893 and is to the design of a Cheshire-born architect, Charles Harrison Townsend, whose most influential work is to be found in London. He designed several other buildings in Blackheath, including Cobbins for himself but in which he is not believed to have lived. Blatchfeld was built for Sir William Roberts-Austen, chemist and assayer and at one time deputy master of the Royal Mint, who, as a lay preacher, held services in a cottage which was incorporated in St Martin's church and is now the vestry. The church, which is side on to the road and can easily be mistaken for a village hall (which is just across the road, in fact), has some interesting murals while outside there is a roll of honour to those local men who lost their lives in the two world wars.

❦ BLETCHINGLEY

The wide A25 cuts a swathe through this charming village which once had a castle and returned two MPs to Westminster. Bletchingley today is much visited. Its tile-hung cottages, along the High Street, and the Whyte Harte Inn ('AD 1388') overlooking the 11th century St Mary's church are the favourite subjects of photographers.

The castle was first mentioned in 1160 and was said to be

one of four in the county. Its life, though, was short as it was destroyed in 1264 during Henry III's war with Simon de Montfort. Men from the garrison were dispatched to Canterbury to guard Thomas à Becket shortly before his martyrdom. Castle Hill and Castle Street at the west end of the village are reminders of the long, gone past.

Cobbett's description of the place as a 'vile rotten borough' came towards the end of Bletchingley's political life. It was electing two Members of Parliament in spite of the fact that the number of voters could almost be counted on the fingers of one's hands. It became a borough in the early 13th century but never had a royal charter. The first MPs were returned in 1285 and the last in 1829, prior to the 1832 Reform Act. Two of the incumbents in the final years of representation in Bletchingley were William Lamb, later Lord Melbourne, PM from 1834-41 and a mentor of young Queen Victoria, and Lord Palmerston.

That Bletchingley has known great times is illustrated in the history of the palace which the Duke of Buckingham built there early in the 16th century. The Duke and Sir Nicholas Carew, who succeeded him, were executed, and the manor came into the hands of Anne of Cleves whose head was spared in spite of her divorce from Henry VIII.

🍁 BLINDLEY HEATH

A prize fight at Blindley Heath in 1815 is believed to have been watched by, among others, the Czar of Russia. He and his entourage stayed at the White Hart in Godstone. Blindley Heath is on the A22 between Godstone and East Grinstead, and to the south of South Godstone where there is a station on the Reading to Tonbridge line via Guildford and Redhill.

🍁 BOOKHAM, GREAT

The National Trust property, Polesden Lacey, was where the Duke and Duchess of York spent their honeymoon. Later, of course, they became the King and Queen of England – George VI and Elizabeth. Polesden Lacey was given to the Trust in 1942 by the Hon Mrs Ronald Greville as a memorial to her father, the Rt Hon William McEwan. The gift comprised the house, the gardens, an estate of 1,000 acres, pictures and other works of art. The present house was begun in 1824, eight years after the original mansion had been pulled down.

The church of St Nicholas is Norman on a Saxon site of worship, and has welcomed many distinguished people into its congregation, not least the future king and queen. An east window is a memorial to Lord Raglan, who lost his life at Sebastopol 40 years after losing an arm at the Battle of Waterloo. The rector from 1769 until his death in 1820 was Jane Austen's godfather, the Rev Samuel Cooke.

The Surrey novelist Fanny Burney lived at a cottage called Fairfield (now The Hermitage) for four years after her marriage to General d'Arblay at Mickleham in 1793. The couple had a child and told the world they were blissfully happy on £125 a year. Fanny wrote *Camilla* while at Great Bookham. Elizabeth Barrett was said to have resided at the Old Rectory; her father rented the property in 1846 in an attempt to get his daughter, who spent much of her time on her back after an injury during childhood, to forget Robert Browning. But as the two poets married in that year and spent much time abroad, it seems that Elizabeth was at Bookham infrequently if at all.

Thomas Briggs, a butcher of Great Bookham, was hanged in January 1594 after being found guilty of breaking into a property at Newdigate and stealing two oxen valued at £8.

🍁 BOOKHAM, LITTLE

The church, whose dedication is unknown, has some 12th century work, and is thought to contain four periods of medieval architecture. The original building comprised only a nave; a south aisle was added around 1160. The north and west walls of this building are still in existence. A tithe barn near the church is probably 15th century and there are a number of 16th century buildings in the village, including the Windsor Castle public house.

🍁 BOURNE, THE

There are three Bournes – Upper, Middle and Lower – which come together as The Bourne, and the prefix is important to local people. The area lies either side of the Bourne stream which starts its life as a Hampshire outflow from Lodge Pond in Alice Holt Forest, then runs along the floor of The Bourne valley before entering the river Wey at Moor Park. It has a short life but the stream has given its name to a beautiful locality and a very fine descriptive writer. George Sturt, wheelwright and countryman, used George Bourne as his *nom de plume* and anyone who reads his books and knows The Bourne can identify the area of the late 19th century. Sturt, born in Farnham in 1863, lived from 1891 in Vine Cottage off Vicarage Hill – still a pine-wooded slope down which the lane falls to cross the stream and run beside a pleasant pub called the Spotted Cow. When he died in 1927, he was buried in the cemetery in Farnham, where a memorial tablet in the parish church reads: 'To the memory of George Sturt of this town who wrote with understanding and distinction of the wheelwright's craft and English peasant life.'

This is also the district of another of England's greatest writers on rural matters, William Cobbett. He received his education here, he said, on a sandhill where, with two of his brothers, he played. 'It is impossible to say how much I owe to that sandhill', he wrote.

Cobbett's sandhills are still there, now heavily wooded and built upon; but it is not too difficult to imagine them as they were more than 200 years ago.

Cobbett was born in the pub that now bears his name in Farnham in 1762, and after his death in 1835, his body was returned to the town for burial. The family tomb is just outside the main door of the parish church.

The Bourne's hub is the crossroads at Lower Bourne where the busy A287 sweeps down Gravel Hill from Farnham, leaving the parish church of St Thomas-on-the-Bourne at the top, and departs for the heaths of Frensham over Gong Hill.

One of the pubs on the main road is the Cricketers which serves as a reminder that the summer game is very important to the village. The ground in Old Frensham Road has seen many a stirring game going back to the days of George Sturt's chairmanship. While the club, in its centenary year, looks to the future with confidence, the Cricketers' days appear to be numbered since an announcement by the brewery, which owns both it and the Fox at the bottom of Gravel Hill, that it wishes to knock it down and sell the land for housing.

In Upper Bourne are two hostelries renowned for their sporting endeavours – the aptly named Bat and Ball and, as befits the area, the Sandrock. They were once in the thick of the hop fields which covered the hillsides south of Farnham. The Bat and Ball was a tally man's office where pickers were given their hard-earned pay, and was transformed into a pub when the pay was augmented by the supply of ale.

🍁 BOWLHEAD GREEN

There are some beautiful lanes between the A3 at Thursley and the A286 at Brook which can lead the traveller to the northern slopes of Hindhead. One passes through the sleepy hamlet of Bowlhead Green where there are some charming buildings, including a former chapel. Congregationalism came to this tiny corner of Surrey in 1865 when the man who owned the chapel, Isaac Kettle, began his ministry. He also toured the district handing out tracts and books, and held regular Sunday afternoon cottage meetings. When he died in 1906 his will revealed that he had bequeathed the building to a relative and services were brought to an abrupt close.

Bowlhead Green is in the parish of Thursley, but is cut off from that village by the A3. The best way to enjoy the hamlet is on foot, either using the Greensand Way, which passes to the north, or by a number of other paths which criss-cross the area and can lead on up to High Button, Hurthill and Gibbet Hill.

❧ Box Hill

The A24 winds around the western side of Box Hill which has been a most favoured beauty spot in the county for centuries. Daniel Defoe observed that an 'abundance of gentlemen and ladies from Epsom [came] to take the air and walk in the box woods'. Nowadays thousands of visitors have turned Box Hill into a very busy place at peak periods. Off-peak, though, it is a good place to be, to wander over the chalky acres and admire the view south across the valley of the Mole as the river meanders through meadows from its source in Sussex. Owned by the National Trust, Box Hill rises to 563ft and is a Site of Special Scientific Interest.

The poet Keats, when a guest at the Burford Bridge Hotel at Westhumble on the western side of Box Hill, claimed that a walk on the hill by moonlight gave him inspiration for part of *Endymion*.

There is a curious memorial on Box Hill which has fascinated visitors for generations. It is the burial place of an eccentric from Dorking, Major Peter Labelliere, an 18th century Marines officer, who demanded that in his final resting position he be upside down so that 'as the world was turned topsy turvy he might come right at last'. The Mad Major had his way, or at least it is presumed he had his way, and millions of people have had a chuckle at his expense.

❧ Bramley

Women's cricket, which has still not been accepted in some quarters in spite of the advances made towards sexual equality, had its birth on Gosden Common beside the road into the village from Guildford. There, in 1745, the maids of Bramley played those from Hambledon, near Godalming, and not, as may be supposed, from the Hampshire village of the same name which will forever be associated with the early age of cricket.

Two years later Bramley's men combined with those from Ripley and Thursley to play London, and another 20 years on a village side was thought good enough to face up to Ripley on the latter's famous cricket green.

Bramley may have few if any other claims to immortality, but its residents have proved themselves to be doughty fighters in recent years with successful campaigns against the imposition of a bail hostel in their midst and the saving of the village school. Both battles were conducted by clearly focused interest groups and were fine examples of people power, epitomising the strength of purpose that can be shown when a community feels threatened.

The village had a station on the Guildford to Brighton railway line which opened in 1865 and closed 100 years later, and there were two mills, one of them at Snowdenham, close to the home of the late Lord Hamilton of Dalzell, who was the Lord Lieutenant of Surrey from 1973-86. Lord Hamilton was the third baron in a line created in 1886, and was related by marriage to the Ricardo family who came to Bramley in Victoria's reign. His eldest son, who lives at Betchworth, is the present Lord Hamilton, while another son, Sir Archibald Hamilton, is the MP for Epsom and Ewell and the chairman of the influential backbench 1922 Committee. Snowdenham was built by the Courage brewery family in 1732.

Guildford Museum has on display tokens given out at Bramley school. There was a round token each week for attendance, punctuality and conduct, and six could be exchanged for an oval-shaped disc with a value of 6d. At the end of each year the 'money' collected was lodged in the child's savings account. The money was given by Col Ricardo who lived at Bramley House from 1886 until the 1930s.

🍁 BROCKHAM

The biggest Guy Fawkes bonfire in Surrey is Brockham's claim. The green by Christ Church is taken over by a massive construction on the morning of the great November celebration, and the village is a place to avoid if you wish to get anywhere in a hurry on the night.

In earlier days Brockham green was a venue for cricket and players of the calibre of Dr W.G. Grace played there. The home players wore straw hats manufactured by the village rush-chair maker, and Eric Parker wrote that when the team went to Mitcham the derisive shout went up: 'Here come the Brockham straw yards.' But the visitors won by an innings to silence the cocky south Londoners.

The village was the home of Captain Morris of the Lifeguards, a 'convivial lyrist', who lived at Brockham Lodge, and died there in 1838 at the age of 93. He was buried at neighbouring Betchworth as Christ Church had not then been built. Brockham became an ecclesiastical parish, separate from St Michael's, Betchworth, in 1848.

In Victorian times there was a Home and Industrial School for the training of orphan girls for domestic services in the village, plus an infant home.

🍁 BROOK

There is an attractive pub, the Dog and Pheasant, in this hamlet on the road between Milford and Haslemere. Opposite, there is a delightful cricket ground. What more could one ask for?

The six-acre ground was a gift to the neighbourhood by the late Viscount Pirrie in 1923, and the hall, which serves as the pavilion and meeting place and which carries the donor's name, was erected in the same year at a cost of £4,000.

Viscount Pirrie, a director of the shipping line that owned the *Titanic*, had bought neighbouring Witley Park in 1905 after it had been seized in the wake of the scandal involving Whitaker Wright.

Witley Park, which is enclosed by six miles of wall, was once known as Lea Park and Cobbett often rested there overnight. The wall – 'the finest in England' was how one newspaper report described it in 1905 – cost £37,000 to build and enclosed 1,400 acres of land. Whitaker Wright, a financier, built the mansion at a cost of £840,000 about 110 years ago and, being the amateur landscaper that he was, spent another half-million on laying out the grounds. Three lakes were dug, and under one he built a glass-roofed ball-room. He even called in Lutyens to lend him a hand. There was also a scheme to turn the park into a racing centre to rival Ascot and Epsom. However, Wright's tenure ended abruptly when he committed suicide in 1904 having swallowed a cyanide capsule while he waited to be taken to prison after being sentenced on fraud charges. He was found guilty of defrauding the London Stock Exchange after two mining companies he claimed to have created were revealed to be works of fiction. Wright had hidden for a fortnight in an ice house on the estate, before making his way to America, from where he was eventually extradited. He was buried in the churchyard at Witley.

Fire seriously damaged Wright's mansion on 10 October 1952. The blaze was tackled by 80 firemen in 13 fire engines, but it destroyed the north wing, including a beautifully panelled ballroom. The mansion had 32 bedrooms, 11 bathrooms, two large dining rooms, a palm court and a number of reception rooms. The present house was built in 1962 and Witley Park is now a privately owned conference centre.

🍁 BROOKWOOD

The cemetery here was well known across the world before the deaths of Diana, Princess of Wales, and her friend, Dodi Fayed, in Paris in 1997. But when Dodi's body was brought to Brookwood for burial, the sprawling cemetery became the focus of intense media activity as a seemingly never-ending stream of mourners and the just plain curious came to pay their last respects to the son of the owner of Harrods. Even when Dodi Fayed's body had been removed to a final resting place on his father's estate at Oxted, the sightseers continued to make their pilgrimage to Brookwood.

The cemetery was opened by Act of Parliament in 1854 after the Necropolis Company of London had bought 2,000 acres of heathland and laid out one-fifth as a burial ground. It had its own railway line with a station in Westminster Road, London, from which a train departed each morning for Brookwood. A crematorium was constructed in 1889. The graves of the rich and the famous are side by side with those of ordinary folk, and cemetery tours are conducted by knowledgeable guides.

It may come as a surprise to know that the Australian fast bowler, Fred Spofforth, whose 14-wicket haul in August 1882, when England were beaten in two days at The Oval, effectively led to the creation of The Ashes, is buried at Brookwood. Spofforth, known as The Demon, was born in Yorkshire in 1853 and taken to Australia as a boy. When he returned to torment the old country, The *Sporting Life* published a mock obituary of English cricket, which ended: 'The body will be cremated and the ashes taken to Australia.' In later life Spofforth returned to England and became a successful businessman in South London. He died in June 1926.

Brookwood Hospital, which was established in 1867 as an asylum for pauper lunatics, has been all but closed over recent years by changes in Government health care policy, and the land sold off for housing and a large superstore.

🍁 BUCKLAND

A gruesome legend is still recounted in these parts. Buckland, a small village between Dorking and Reigate, is known now for its picturesque pond and group of buildings beside the A25, but in pre-Victorian times it was some kind of water monster that made people talk.

The 'thing' – ape-like by all accounts – was known as the Buckland Shag and lived near a stone by a stream. An article in *The Gentleman's Magazine* in 1827 opened: 'The road from Reigate to Dorking leads through a lonely lane, of considerable length, into the village of Buckland. In the most obscure part of this lane a little stream of beautifully clear water crosses the way. By the side of this very stream laid a large stone for I know not how many years – perhaps for centuries.'

The apparition used to appear at midnight and in that 19th century piece were two instances of a person or persons coming face to face with the beast. A Buckland man was returning from Reigate market, the worse for wear, when he entered the lane and saw it. He hit out with his stick but made no impression. He sobered up in a flash and, chased by the ghost, set off for his cottage. When at last he reached his door, he collapsed and was helped to his bed where he died a week later. On another occasion a wagon and four horses reached the spot and would go no further even though the stream was only two feet wide and its depth perfectly manageable.

The Church of Our Lady was rebuilt in 1860. Three hundred years earlier the churchyard was the scene of an offence which had its climax in the assizes. Thomas Dalender, gent., of Buckland was indicted for drawing his sword in the churchyard with the intention of assaulting John Alleayne, a yeoman of the village. History neither records whether Alleayne was injured nor the verdict returned against Dalender.

Buckland today has sand and gravel pits, a delightful green and pond, beside which stands an old barn with a turret – and a property called Shagbrook which stands as a reminder to those who know of the legend of the village.

❧ BURPHAM

This once rural village has all but been swallowed up by developers. There are large housing estates and Guildford's first out-of-town superstore where once there were green fields. Years ago Burpham was distant enough from Guildford for town dwellers to walk through Stoke Park to the village, slake their thirst at the Green Man, and return home again. Now, London Road is continuous building and a very busy thoroughfare, in spite of the close proximity of Guildford's second bypass in half a century which was designed to alleviate places such as Burpham from the daily pressure associated with the motor car.

The Green Man has always been the focal point of the village, and will presumably continue to fulfil that role for a long time to come, since in 1593 it was the subject of a 1,000-year lease and the freehold was claimed in the 1970s. The pub was rebuilt at the beginning of the century and underwent substantial change in the 1980s when it became part of a popular restaurant chain. Attached to it is the Paddock Room, which was a 19th century private house when it was acquired by the brewers in 1930. Nearer Guildford is the Anchor and Horseshoes which became a public house in the 19th century, and probably got the second part of its name from the fact that there were stables and a blacksmith's forge on or about the site in earlier times.

Burpham's little church of St Luke, standing above the new A3, was built in 1859 by the Surrey architect Henry Woodyer and renovated as its centenary was celebrated.

🍁 BURSTOW

This village near the Sussex border means only one thing to me: the birthplace of the great 19th century cricketer William Lambert. Known to his contemporaries as the finest batsman of his age, Lambert was born in 1779 and died in 1851. He lived much of his life in nearby Nutfield, where he was a miller and had an involvement in the fuller's earth trade, but was buried in the churchyard of St Bartholomew's at Burstow.

Lambert was the first player to score a century in both innings of a match at the present Lord's ground, when playing for Sussex against Epsom – a curious fixture by today's standards. He made 107 not out in the first innings and 157 in the second, and it was 76 years later before the feat was next achieved, by A.E. Stoddart who made 195 not out and 124 for Middlesex against Nottingham. Lambert's feat was in 1817 and that was a year that turned sour for him as he was 'warned off the turf' at Lord's for allegedly not playing his best – 'selling the match' – in England v Nottinghamshire.

So William Lambert, who the previous year had appeared as the author of a manual entitled *Instructions and Rules for playing the Noble Game of Cricket* was drummed out. But he continued to play cricket in the country, especially in Surrey, and his last match was recorded as being in 1839.

Burstow does not appear to have a heart. Perhaps it has been ripped out by the jets which fly into and out of nearby Gatwick Airport, or by the M23 which is even closer. The church, though, is in very rural surroundings. It dates from around 1120 and has a wooden tower and shingle spire. One of its incumbents was John Flamsteed, who was created the first Astronomer Royal by Charles II. He held the living from 1684 until he died in 1719. It is said he was buried in the chancel. While at Burstow he and Sir Isaac Newton worked on and disputed astronomical subjects. As Eric Parker observed, it was quite an achievement to be made Astronomer Royal when Newton was alive.

❧ BUSBRIDGE

The great gardener Gertrude Jekyll was buried in the church-yard at St John the Baptist in Busbridge in 1932. She had spent many years of her life at Munstead, just south of Busbridge on the way out of Godalming, and Jekyll devotees will know the area well. It is not only her garden designs, many of which have been faithfully followed or restored, but her collaboration with the architect Sir Edwin Lutyens that makes this area of South West Surrey so appealing. Miss Jekyll's mother and brother and sister-in-law are also buried at St John the Baptist, which was designed by George Gilbert Scott junior.

Thirty years after Miss Jekyll's death, another gardener, but of an entirely different kind, was also buried in the church-yard. Dr Wilfrid Fox was the creator of nearby Winkworth Arboretum, now owned by the National Trust. He was the senior consultant at St George's Hospital in London and the outstanding dermatologist of his age when, in 1938, he bought Winkworth Farm at Hascombe, together with 100 acres of scrub-covered hillside, and in time decided to create a place of beauty and tranquillity (see also Hascombe). Dr Fox died in 1962.

Busbridge Hall, a late 18th century house demolished in 1906 and replaced, is a wildfowl centre which draws many visitors. Crowds of a different kind travelled there in days gone by to watch leading cricketers, including overseas tourists, in action.

🍁 BYFLEET

Brooklands, that famed home of early motor sport, is close to what is left of Byfleet's village identity. The track, with its steep banking, part of which has been reconstructed, was built in

Lock cottage, circa 1780, New Haw, near Byfleet.

1907 by Hugh Locke King, a motoring and aeronautics pioneer. In 1909 he opened an aerodrome in the middle of the 2.75-mile circuit. Vickers Armstrong took it over in 1936 and it was the site of important military innovations in the Second World War, including the Wellington bomber and the bouncing bomb designed by Barnes Wallis. The spirit of Brooklands is captured at its museum where, situated in many of the original buildings, is a wonderful collection of items which evoke the memory of the days of early motor racing and flying. Motor-racing continued there until the outbreak of the Second World War, but never returned, and the focus, when hostilities had ended, switched to an old wartime airfield in Northamptonshire. Silverstone was born. However, Brooklands could never be forgotten, because so much of what is taken for granted in the world of motor sport and aeronautics had its origins at Locke King's concrete racetrack.

A Bronze Age bucket and a hoard of Roman coins which were dug up in Byfleet are in the British Museum. The church of St Mary the Virgin is late 13th century, and one of its 18th century rectors was Stephen Duck, who had earlier made the transition from Wiltshire labourer to Beefeater to the Queen and Keeper of a royal library at Richmond. He learned Latin and was ordained but in a fit of melancholy drowned himself in the Thames.

Royal Manor House was a royal hunting lodge but is now private apartments. Edward II stayed there frequently; the Black Prince lived there and stabled his horses at nearby Wisley; and legend has it that Henry VIII was nursed there as a baby. The house was rebuilt by Anne of Denmark but has since been reconstructed to such an extent that were she to return she would recognise only the gate pillars, which are listed.

B. Hawkins

Byfleet Manor, Surrey.

🍁 CAPEL

Capel is a small village south of Dorking which was named after a capella or chapel that was used for worship in the 11th century.

The present church is largely 13th century and was originally dedicated to St Lawrence. Five hundred years later it was rededicated to St John the Baptist.

The parish once had a curate who wrote a charm against toothache – and was probably thanked many times over in the days before the dentist's chair.

There is an old legend that if you walk around the churchyard yew here one hundred times at midnight a ghost will appear. What a pity that so few supernatural legends are as easy to verify!

The founder of the Quaker movement, George Fox, visited Capel in 1668 because of the district's involvement in the religion. It was brought to Capel by the Bax family in 1655 and Pleystowe, the house of Richard Bax, became home and local headquarters to the followers.

🍁 CATERHAM

Caterham-on-the-Hill will be remembered, not always with affection, by the guardsmen who passed through the former barracks. The depot was built in 1877 along with St Lawrence's Hospital and they were forerunners of what is now a busy community. After a long debate about the future of the 60-acre military depot, which the Ministry of Defence sold to a property developer, it appears that a mix of residential and business buildings will rise from the site in a so-called 'urban village'. Caterham Valley grew up when the railway arrived in

1856 and the shepherds and quarrymen were gradually eased out. The old parish church of St Lawrence dates from Norman times and was disused from 1866, when St Mary's was built opposite, until 1927 when it was reopened. The area is now part of Tandridge District Council, which was formed by a merger of Caterham and Warlingham Urban District Council and Godstone Rural District Council. Tandridge is the most easterly of Surrey's ten district authorities and shares with Mole Valley the distinction of not being a borough and thus not having a mayor.

❧ CATTESHALL

The riverside area to the east of Godalming has for centuries been dominated by the mill at Catteshall. It is thought to be one of three Godalming mills recorded in the Domesday Book – the others being Westbrook and Eashing – and has been thoroughly researched by local industrial archaeologists Alan and Glenys Crocker. The mill stands beside the road which winds through Catteshall, and beside the river which forms part of the National Trust's Wey Navigation and runs through Godalming's historic open space known as the Lammas Lands. The research has been part of the work undertaken on the restoration of the mill's water turbine which is said to be the largest and best preserved example in the country, and one of Surrey's most significant industrial monuments.

Corn milling, malting, fulling, paper making, tanning, engineering, and foundry work have all been carried out at Catteshall. A significant date is 1838 when Thomas Sweetapple patented his invention of 'an improvement or improvements in the machinery for paper making'. Paper had been made in continuous rolls since 1803, and Sweetapple's improvements gave Catteshall a new lease of life through to the 20th century when Albert Reed, whose name is synonymous with paper making, became the owner of what was then called Farncombe Paper Mills. Paper made at Catteshall was used by the *News of the World* and leading motoring and motor-cycle journals. Reed continued to operate there until the 1930s depression when 100 local mill workers lost their jobs, and it was not until 1939 that engineers and founders took over the place.

There was Government work for 300 people during the war, but as peace returned the orders dwindled and only one-tenth of the wartime workforce was required by the 1970s. The mill was again sold and the present owners have helped with the preservation of equipment, including the turbine which had been installed in 1870.

Unsted Park is in the Catteshall locality, a late 18th century house which was built as Farley Hill. Memories of a downstairs maid at Unsted were published in the *Surrey Advertiser* in 1984. 'The working quarters were the basement,' recalled the writer, 'and we never saw daylight. To me it was an immense place. They seemed to have endless servants. I never did see all of them. In my domain were capacious sinks and a large furnace which was lit by the odd job man, but I was warned if this went out I had to relight it, so I kept the blessed thing stoked up. The prospect of relighting it filled me with dismay so I made the water so hot it bubbled away and reached boiling point. When I started running it, it scalded my fingers which was the cause of my leaving.'

The period was just after the First World War, and the former maid continued: 'Besides loads of washing up and endless wide passages to keep clean with hearthstone, there were the copper saucepans to keep bright and clean, and that was a nightmare. After washing them I had to clean the insides with sand and the outsides with salt and vinegar to remove stains, and polish them afterwards. The only time I had off was every other Sunday afternoon when I finished all the washing up.' And she added: 'I worked from 5.30 am till late at night in dim light, and no fresh air, and it affected me.'

🍁 CHALDON

Close to the North Downs Way and the Greater London border, Chaldon attracts thousands of visitors because of a discovery made more than 120 years ago. It was in 1870 that workmen renovating the 11th century church of St Peter uncovered a wall painting which sent experts and others into Victorian ecstasy.

The 12th century painting measures 17ft 2in by 11ft 2in and is 'archaeologically at least ... the most valuable and interesting wall painting in England'. It has as its theme the Ladder of Salvation. Its preservation was due to the rector at the time, the Rev H. Shepherd, who kept an eye on the work and 'catching sight of some colour peeping out beneath the whitewash, warned those employed in removing the latter and thus preserved the painting from being destroyed', stated the Surrey Archaeological Society.

There is a plaque in the church with the following inscription:

'Good Redar warne all men and women while they be here to
be ever
good to the poore and the nedy.
The cry of the poore is extreme and very sore.
In thys worlde we rune oure rase.
God graunt us to be with Christ in tyme and space.'

And there is a bell in the porch which is thought to have been cast as early as 1250.

Chaldon has a few old farms and a collection of more recent houses. It remains a fairly isolated community. It has had a history of water problems; the supply even into the 20th century was recorded as being small and intermittent and apt to fail in summer when the residents were dependent on shallow wells and ponds.

🍁 CHARLWOOD

This border village has undergone as much change as any in the county because of the phenomenal growth of Gatwick Airport. London's second airport is at the village's back door, and the only thing that comes between the two of them is the county boundary. For while Gatwick has been transferred to Sussex, Charlwood has successfully fought tooth and nail to remain in Surrey.

Before the big jets came to disturb the area, Charlwood was just a sleepy, peaceful village. Eric Parker, though, noted that it was being 'stiffened and discoloured' by building contractors as early as the first decade of the 20th century, and while a village can to a point withstand the 'improvements' carried out by the building trade it surely cannot beat off the jet engine.

The Brighton road through the parish was part of the first road in Surrey to be made under the Turnpike Act in the reign of William III. But it was not until George II was on the throne that it became a 'driving road'. Gatwick racecourse was a well patronised place around the turn of the century after the track at Croydon had closed.

Agnes Dye's pregnancy probably saved her from the gallows in Elizabeth I's reign. The Charlwood spinster was found guilty in 1562 of the theft of 50s in money, a petticoat cloth valued at 13s 4d, and a sheet worth 5s. When she appeared before the judge he observed that she was with child and remanded her to jail where she remained until the following January when she was freed in a general pardon. Eleven years later another Agnes of Charlwood – it could even have been the same one – appeared in an Elizabethan sex scandal. Agnes Wood, a widow, was the mistress of one John Davie, a shoemaker, of Charlwood, who was charged with the rape of 10-year-old Anne Wood in the house of Agnes, and was found not guilty at Croydon Assizes.

🍁 CHELSHAM

From St Leonard's church it was said you could see the Crystal Palace and the Greenwich Observatory. Chelsham is high up on the slopes of North East Surrey and close to the boundary with Greater London. Buried in the churchyard is Thomas Kelly who looked after his father's sheep on Scotshall Farm when he was a boy, went to London at the age of 14 in 1786, became a publisher and eventually, in 1836, the Lord Mayor. The local boy who made good is remembered in the church by the Kelly Bible and Prayer Book. Kelly, who is buried under a yew tree, provided in his will for the distribution in Chelsham of a quartern loaf of bread on a particular Sunday, a benefaction to the priest who preaches on that day, and a gift for the school.

🍁 CHIDDINGFOLD

In the Middle Ages, Chiddingfold was a great glass-making centre. There were eleven glass works on the village green in the reign of Elizabeth I, and the residents wanted them suppressed because they were a nuisance. Modern Chiddingfold knows nothing of glass-making, but some of its residents complained in the 1980s about a 20th century industry: oil. When the welldiggers moved on to the rather oddly named Penang Farm some people had visions of a real-life Dallas on their doorstep. But the black gold was not found.

Chiddingfold is the largest of the Fold villages and draws thousands of visitors to its pretty centre where the green, pond, church, old houses and 14th century Crown Inn come together. It is not difficult to imagine life back in the glass-making heyday. Chiddingfold has a timeless quality to it even though traffic rushes through its heart. Glass from the village went into St Stephen's Chapel at Westminster in 1351 and a few years later Edward III called for the best glass Chiddingfold could provide when he was building St George's Chapel at Windsor.

The Winterton Arms pub to the north of the village recalls the Earls of Winterton whose seat was at Shillinglee, just over the county border in West Sussex. Shillinglee was the scene of great cricket matches in the middle of the 19th century (the ground is now part of a golf course) and Lord Winterton was an opening bat. In September 1847 he was playing against Farnham when a ball bowled by Frederick Caesar killed a swallow as it swooped across the pitch. His lordship also played for Chiddingfold, two of whose players at that time became prominent enough to have their obituary notices published in Wisden. One was Alfred Hoar, who left the village as a teenager to become a professional player. The other was James Sadler, who was a member of a prominent Chiddingfold family. Wisden recorded in 1925: 'Like his father and grandfather, he was a lover of the game. In his early days he had been invited to play for the county, but he preferred to restrict his activities to local matches in the West Surrey district. His death caused many interesting links with the past to be severed. He was, it is believed, the last survivor of the Shillinglee team which dismissed the Second Royal Surrey Militia without a run on August 13, 1855. For over 20 years he knew the great William

Beldham well, and as a small child he had met Tom Walker, another member of the famous Hambledon XI, who died as long ago as 1831.'

James Charyngham was a Chiddingfold butcher who went to the gallows in Elizabeth I's reign because he stole a heifer valued at eight shillings. He was sentenced at Southwark Sessions on 7 November 1560, after being found guilty of stealing the animal at night from a fellow villager, John Whyte.

Bonfire night is always a big occasion in Chiddingfold, with thousands celebrating in traditional style. Once, in 1929, the fire was set alight prematurely and the angry scenes which followed led to 250 police officers being sent to the village and a Justice of the Peace prepared to read the Riot Act.

🍁 CHILWORTH

Six men were killed in an explosion at the gunpowder works in Chilworth in February 1901. 'The most terrible accident which it has ever been our painful duty to record,' said the *Surrey Advertiser*. The explosion, soon after the men's breakfast break on a Tuesday, blasted the two-storey Black Corning House to pieces. It signalled the end of the village's long association with the manufacture of gunpowder.

There had been other explosions; one in 1763 brought down the tower of St Martha's church on top of the hill above the mill. Chilworth and gunpowder were together as early as 1580, but the Chilworth Gunpowder Company was not formed until 1885. Cobbett knew them and detested them. He thought the vale of Chilworth was 'exquisitely beautiful' and 'seems to have been created by a bountiful providence as one of the choicest retreats of man' but 'has been, by ungrateful man, so perverted as to make it instrumental in effecting two of the most damnable of purposes, namely the making of gunpowder and banknotes! Here, in this tranquil spot, where the nightingales are to be heard earlier and later in the year than in any other part of England; where the first bursting of the buds is seen in spring, where no rigours of season can ever be felt; where everything seems formed for precluding the very thought of wickedness; here has the devil fixed as one of the seats of his grand manufactory; and perverse and ungrateful man not only lends him his aid, but lends it cheerfully!'

Cobbett's broadside did not stop production. As many as 400 people were employed in the mills at their peak. The paper mill burnt down at the end of the 19th century. There was a mill listed in the Domesday Book and corn and fulling mills were situated in Chilworth in 1589. In Charles I's reign the East India Company set up more extensive mills in the locality.

What is left of a once prosperous industry can be seen in an attractive walk through the area where interpretation boards help to give a better understanding of the work that went on in the Tillingbourne valley.

Chilworth today is a quiet village where history is unlikely to repeat itself. It has its fair share of visitors because of the hilltop church of St Martha, rebuilt by Henry Woodyer, the Surrey architect, in 1850. The earliest documentary evidence of the name is around 1200, and in 1463 Bishop Waynflete of Winchester wrote of 'the chapel dedicated to Saint Martha the Virgin and all the Holy Martyrs, commonly called Martirhill founded and situated next to the town of Guldeforde in our diocese'. There is, according to the chaplain in a letter to the *Surrey Advertiser* in 1984, a strong tradition that early Christians were martyred there by pagan Saxons about AD 600 as part of the resistance movement to the spread of Christianity. If this were true, he wrote, then Martha could be a corruption of Martyr. 'Those of us connected with the church believe that the dedication of St Martha originated in Norman times and was a deliberate choice,' he added.

🍁 CHIPSTEAD

The man who rose from labourer in the quarries at Merstham to be the builder of London Bridge is commemorated in Chipstead's 12th century church of St Margaret. Sir Edward Banks is said to have first observed the 'pleasant situation' of Chipstead when working on the railway at Merstham in 1803. Before he died in 1835 he had also constructed the bridges across the Thames at Waterloo and Southwark, and built the naval dockyard at Sheerness.

Peter Aubertin was the rector of Chipstead for 50 years and the story is told of what he discovered on his arrival in 1809. His predecessor had lived in Croydon and St Margaret's was in a rundown state. Cricketers used it as a pavilion where they drank beer and ate bread and cheese and, it is recorded, even notched the runs into the wood of the altar. The new incumbent, mostly by his own hands, restored the church, even painting the glass in the windows and catching the experts off-guard when they tried to date the work.

🍁 CHOBHAM

A 'grand military picnic' was held on Chobham Common in 1853 but it turned out to be the start of something more serious, for from that exercise came the decision to establish Aldershot as the Home of the British Army. Queen Victoria reviewed the troops at Chobham on 21 June 1853, and in 1901 a cross was put on the spot to mark the occasion and at the same time act as a memorial to the late monarch.

The camp was held from April until August and, said a writer of the period, was sufficient to prove the need for a more permanent school for field operations where officers might

Brook Place, Chobham, built in 1656.

learn to handle large bodies of men and where the men might learn to rough it, and to draw more upon their own ingenuity for comfort.

Chobham Common and Ridges have remained as military training grounds and are about five miles from the village where, in the early 19th century, there was a pig auction on Sunday mornings before church on land between the churchyard and the White Hart. St Lawrence's church dates back 800 years although it has been heavily restored. One of its monuments is to Sir Edward Banks who built Waterloo, Southwark and London Bridges. There is the tomb of Nicholas Heath, Archbishop of York from 1556-60, and Lord Chancellor of England under Queen Mary. He died in the Tower in 1578. He was described as an 'upright and brave man firm in his own convictions but tolerant of the religious opinions of others'. He refused to conform to the Elizabethan changes and resigned his See and went to live at Chobham Park which he had bought from Queen Mary for £3,000.

At the time of the Domesday survey Chobham, or Cebeha, was held by Chertsey Abbey which had been founded as early as the seventh century. A church was recorded but no mills, although there is evidence of three such buildings on The Bourne brook.

🍁 CHURT

Cobbett's plan to pass through Churt on a wild November night in 1822 came to nought when his guide became hopelessly lost. Today's travellers need have no fears for Churt is a modern village with a busy main road. However, get away from the A287 and there are many pleasant lanes and footpaths.

The hub of the village is the crossroads and the Crossways pub – one of the few inns in this south-west corner of the county which has altered little over the years. It was known at one stage as The Shant, supposedly on account of the landlady's repeated negative replies to proposals by her customers. One mile away is the Pride of the Valley inn, where the sign shows another pride of the valley, David Lloyd George, whose house, Bron-y-de, was close by. The fiery Welsh statesman was living in Churt in 1943 when he married his long-time secretary Frances Stevenson.

Lloyd George moved to Churt in 1921 and built Bron-y-de which is, alas, no more. His successful experiments in farming and fruit growing made him a popular figure in local agricultural circles, and he and his wife were in demand to put in appearances at shows and fetes. He is still remembered by older folk, many of whom worked on his estate.

Frensham Pond is fed by streams which come down through Churt. One flows from the slopes of Hindhead, past the Pride of the Valley and on to Silverbeck, near the junction of Jumps Road and the A287, on the corner of which was the old village post office. Another feeder stream flows from Hampshire into Surrey at Whitmoor Vale and continues on through Barford where there were at least three mills straddling the county boundary. Nowadays, it is a cut-off part of the village, known only to the few residents, ramblers and horseriders. Jack Hillier in his book, *Old Surrey Watermills*, stated that a corn mill operated at Barford until the Great War, and that downstream there was a paper mill. But all of this has been lost in the mists of time, as has the area known as Upper Churt Common where, said Harry Baker in his *Frensham Then and Now*, ponies grazed in large numbers. The common began at Hatch Hill, where the road up from Churt ended at a gateway, and extended through what is now built-up Hindhead, across the Portsmouth road to Pitfold which was once the southern boundary of Frensham parish. There were herds of

Heron at Churt.

57

fallow deer, and it was the home of the black cock and grey hen, more commonly known as black grouse. According to Harry Baker, the area around what is now the golf course at Hindhead – founded in the early part of the 20th century and with Sir Arthur Conan Doyle as its president – was one of the favourite haunts of the black grouse. The birds were numerous on the heaths and moors of southern England but now they do not breed further south than Staffordshire. An interesting fact is that where conifers have been planted in vast quantities the black grouse has been making a comeback. Could they make a reappearance in Surrey as conifer replaces broadleaf in some areas?

As we see more parcels of land being turned over to conifers it is easy to imagine a decline in deciduous woodland, but this is untrue, according to the Forestry Commission. In a paper entitled *Broadleaves in Britain* in 1984, it was stated that there had been no appreciable change in the area of broadleaved woodland over the previous 30 years.

Churt's playing field is a First World War memorial, and before that the cricketers played near Frensham Pond where the captain often had difficulty getting all his players ready for the match. They lingered in the nearby hotel and it was not until a barrel of beer was taken to the ground that the skipper was sure of having eleven players present, but perhaps not always correct, at the appointed starting time.

🍁 CLANDON, EAST

Once called Clandon Abbots, East Clandon has the ancient church of St Thomas of Canterbury which was a stopping-off place for pilgrims on their way to Kent. There is also the National Trust house, Hatchlands, which was built in 1758 by Admiral Edward Boscawen, a naval hero, 'at the expense of the enemies of his country', according to his tombstone in his native Cornwall. Boscawen died in 1761, but not before he had given the architect Robert Adam his first commission in England. Hatchlands was given to the National Trust in 1947, and the present tenant is Alec Cobbe, a picture restorer and collector of musical instruments, which are on show at the house.

Between East and West Clandon, wrote Eric Parker, 'the road runs by what is surely the finest ploughland in the county. A single field of over 100 acres stretches up the side of the down to a belt of firs.' Clandon Downs rise to the top of Newlands Corner and agriculture is still the predominant use.

🍁 CLANDON, WEST

West Clandon is nearer to Guildford, but far enough away for its houses to be much sought after by people looking for a home in the country which is within reach of the town and close to both rail and road links to London. Clandon Park is the home of the Onslow family who came from Shropshire in 1642 in the person of Sir Richard Onslow. Three members of the family have risen to the position of Speaker of the House of Commons. The house was built by the Venetian architect Giacomo Leoni in 1731, and the grounds were laid out by 'Capability' Brown.

West Clandon, which has been known as Clandon Regis and King's Clandon, has an attractive, winding main street along which is the low ceilinged Onslow Arms and the church of St Peter and St Paul. The latter is built on the site of a Domesday church and John Aubrey observed that it had fallen down 'a small time before Xmas in 1716'. It was not completely destroyed and was rebuilt 'by the contributions of parishioners'.

Stories of the serpent at West Clandon are still told. *The Gentleman's Magazine* in 1796 carried the following account: 'A serpent once infested a back lane in the parish of West Clandon for a long time. The inhabitants were much disturbed and afraid to pass that way. A soldier who had been condemned for desertion promised, if his life was spared, he would destroy this serpent. Accordingly he took his dog with him. A fierce battle ensued, the dog fastened him and the soldier killed it with his bayonet in a field belonging to the glebe called Deadacre.' There is a carving at the church which purports to depict the engagement.

🍁 CLAYGATE

When the common at Claygate was enclosed in 1838 residential expansion soon followed, and when the railway came in 1885 the building boom really took off. Claygate is close to the Greater London boundary and therefore popular with commuters. The church of Holy Trinity was consecrated by the Bishop of Winchester in December 1840, local residents having built it when they found the nearest church at Thames Ditton too far away for regular worship. The A3 sweeps around the east of Claygate, and travellers have a view of Ruxley Towers which was built in the 1830s as a country house and is now offices. During the Second World War, Ruxley Towers was the headquarters of the NAAFI when it was evacuated from London.

🍁 COBHAM

Some would argue that Cobham is no longer a village, and they would probably be correct. In recent years there has been

THE SURREY VILLAGE BOOK ▪ COBHAM

a housing boom and the old place is not the same. But Cobham of yesteryear is remembered fondly by the older members of the community. The broad sweep of the A3 by the White Lion public house and on up to Esher past the extensive grounds of the Fairmile Hotel are fading memories for motorists. Now, drivers rush past Cobham without hardly knowing it is there, carried on their way by a six-lane bypass.

The bridge over the river Mole, which once carried the main Portsmouth road, was reputed to have been built for Queen Matilda, who died in 1118. She was the wife of Henry I and the river crossing was said to be in memory of one of her servants who drowned there. Rather improbable, as the construction date is 1351, but in any case the bridge was rebuilt in 1782 to the design of the county surveyor of the time, George Gwilt.

Matthew Arnold, poet, critic, philosopher, lived in Cobham, at Painshill Cottage, from 1873-1888. Arnold was also a school inspector which befits the son of Dr Thomas Arnold, the legendary headmaster of Rugby School in *Tom Brown's Schooldays*. Painshill Park was created by Charles Hamilton, youngest son of the sixth Earl of Abercorn. Two presidents of the United States, Jefferson and Adams, were among the thousands of visitors who came out from London to wonder at Hamilton's work. Over the years the park became neglected but now, thanks to a preservation society, it has been returned to something like its former glory.

Cobham made the front page of the *Daily Mirror* in 1938 when a puritanical local councillor claimed that 'orgies' at local hops rivalled Sodom and Gomorrah. 'Dance morals trial held up by roars of village', screamed the *Mirror* in typical fashion. Girls and boys were 'cuddling and kissing in dark corners', alleged the councillor. 'Rubbish', stormed the indignant locals at a hearing in the village. The elected representative was given a rough ride and eventually the young people of the village were vindicated. The hoo-haa soon died down.

Two miles south-west of Cobham is the Hatchford mausoleum on Wisley Common, a domed temple erected by Sir Bernhard Samuelson in 1906. The copper top was stolen from the tomb in 1961.

🍁 COLDHARBOUR

Leith Hill is the highest point in Surrey – at 967ft it tops Gibbet Hill at Hindhead by 72ft. And the tower on the summit rounds up the height to exactly 1,000ft – a mountain in Surrey! The tower was built around 1765 by Richard Hull of Leith Hill Place. It comprised two rooms and a staircase, and when Mr Hull died in 1772 he was buried underneath and, if one story is to be believed, upside down so he might face his Maker the right way up.

The tower was vandalised and became the haunt of so-called undesirable characters until, in 1796, it was filled with stones and cement. It remained that way until 1862 when it was restored, and is today, thanks to the National Trust, a popular place with visitors.

Writing in the 17th century, Aubrey saw the 'whole county of Sussex, as far as the South Downes, and even beyond them to the sea; this entire county, part of Hampshire, Berkshire, and Nettlebed in Oxfordshire; some parts of Buckinghamshire, Hertfordshire, Middlesex, Kent and Essex; and by the help of a telescope, Wiltshire. It is much the highest eminence in this county (which has many other Alpes). The whole circumference cannot be less than 200 miles, far exceeding that of the keep and terrass at Windsor Castle, over which (as also the City of London, 25 miles distant) one sees as far as the eye, unarmed with art, is able to distinguish land from sky. The like, I think, is not to be found in any part of England, or perhaps Europe, beside.'

Ordnance surveyors in 1844 recorded 41 spires of London churches from the summit of Leith Hill which is close to Coldharbour, a small village at 750ft and therefore one of the highest in the county. The King's High Way, the old London to Arundel road, passed through Coldharbour, and on Gallows Hill criminals from the assizes at Dorking were hanged in the 17th century. Much earlier there was an Iron Age camp at Anstiebury which was again used during the Napoleonic wars to shelter women and children from Dorking while the men fought the French.

🍁 COMPTON

'Of the 25 parishes in England which bear the name of Compton, probably there is not one which can surpass Compton in Surrey in simple rural beauty, or in the interesting character of its church, an edifice which possesses the unique feature of a double sanctuary and also enshrines the oldest piece of Norman woodwork known in England.' That description appeared in volume XII of the Surrey Archaeological Collections following visits by members of the Surrey Archaeological Society in 1855 and 1861.

Compton's 'simple rural beauty' still exists in spite of the close proximity of the A3 and also a busy main street. The church of St Nicholas is in a secluded corner, and has been described as the best of its style in England. It is approached from the east by a path which runs through a well tended churchyard whose level has been raised dramatically by burials in the 800 years before the village's present cemetery was consecrated in 1905.

The village has become well known for its connections with the painter George Frederic Watts, who lived at Limnerslease in Down Lane. After he died in 1904, his widow, Mary, built a

The memorial building to George Frederic Watts.

memorial chapel and cloister on top of a hill overlooking the village. The striking red-brick chapel is built in the shape of a Greek cross and is reached by a winding, tree-lined climb. Beyond is the cloister where Watts is buried. The hillside has become the village burial ground and there can be few more impressively situated last resting places in the county. Near to Limnerslease, which was built for Watts in 1891, is a Lutyens bridge which carried until recently the A3 Guildford bypass over the Pilgrims' Way. In the vicinity are tunnels in the chalk of the North Downs but the entrances have long been blocked up.

Just along the lane from the chapel is the Watts Gallery which houses many of the artist's works. That lane climbs to the eastern end of the Hog's Back and offers extensive views across Godalming, with the spires of Charterhouse School standing out above the trees, to Hindhead and Blackdown.

At this point there is a gap in the North Downs which has been spanned by a bridge carrying traffic from the A3 on to the Hog's Back. Nothing strange about that, except that gipsies claim they have put a curse on the structure. Certainly, the original bridge was plagued by structural problems from the time it was built in the late 1970s, and in recent times the crossing was closed for many months while engineers carried out major strengthening work.

At the Watts Gallery there is also a tea room which is popular with walkers on the North Downs Way, which comes in from Puttenham under the Lutyens bridge and goes on to Guildford.

We will finish this piece as we began, with a quotation from the S.A.C. It is an extract from a petition to the House of Commons in 1640 that the vicar of Godalming be summoned to answer for his behaviour. One paragraph reads: 'That the said vicar and Mr Wayferar, Parson of Compton, in the said Countie of Surry, roade to Southampton, to eate Fishe and to make merrie together, and there (dyverse tymes) drank healthes to the Pope calling him that honest olde man.'

🍁 Cox Green

This is brick-making country close to the county boundary with West Sussex, where some of the oldest houses in the county are situated, many of them tile-hung with picturesque gardens. Cox Green residents have fought hard to keep their part of Ewhurst parish in Surrey. Their homes are so close to Rudgwick and West Sussex, and in 1987 the Boundary Commission published proposals that, if accepted, would have moved 33 houses out of Surrey and Waverley borough and into West Sussex and Horsham district. The inhabitants feared over-development and the phrase 'suburban metroland' was coined, which sounded like something John Betjeman might have talked about. The residents formed an association and put their faith in a covenant drawn up in 1934 which was discovered quite by chance during a search of the deeds of one of the houses. The covenant stated that only one property

THE SURREY VILLAGE BOOK ■ CRANLEIGH

could be built on any one of eight given plots, whereas planning permission had been sought for two dwellings on one of the plots.

Cox Green remains in Surrey and quite isolated from the rest of the parish, although only a stone's throw from the county boundary.

🍁 CRANLEIGH

The locals proudly claim Cranleigh to be a village; some even say it is the largest in the country. In truth it is a town which retains some village charm. It was once a centre of the iron industry in Surrey and the Weald.

Cranleigh Common, where cricket is played and, until it moved to Cranleigh School in 1997, a week-long tennis tournament was held every year, is close to the heart of the main shopping centre. Beside the common stands a hotel whose name is a reminder that Cranleigh was spelt Cranley until the post office, around the turn of the century, decided there was too much confusion for their staff with Crawley in Sussex.

Cranleigh, named after the cranes and herons formerly found on ponds at Baynards and Vachery, was on the Guildford to Brighton line, but following its closure in 1965, as a result of Dr Beeching's cuts, the station was demolished and redeveloped. The railway ran through delightful countryside, much of which is now available to ramblers and riders, and passed through the station at Baynards before leaving the county.

The first cottage hospital in England was opened at Cranleigh in 1859. Cranleigh Village Hospital was founded in October of that year by Albert C. Napper MRCS, LSA, with assistance from the local rector, Archdeacon J.H. Sapte, who donated rent-free a small cottage which originally housed six beds and an operating room. Mr Napper practised in Cranleigh from 1854 to 1881 and had previously been in Guildford. Archdeacon Sapte was the incumbent at St Nicholas's church from 1846 to 1906. It is said that the cleric's gift was prompted by an emergency when Mr Napper had to amputate a man's leg in a nearby cottage after an accident in Cranleigh.

Cranleigh School was founded in 1864 and originally catered for 26 sons of farmers. It became a public school in 1898 and will soon admit girls from the age of thirteen.

🍁 CROWHURST

Queen Victoria and Prince Albert are reputed to have made a special visit from Windsor to view the wonder of this rural village: the yew tree in the churchyard. Surrey has so many gnarled old yew trees, each claiming to be famous, but the one at Crowhurst is arguably the king of them all. So it was most appropriate that the Queen of England should honour it with a visit.

The yew, which some say is 1,500 years old, stands close to St George's church on a hilltop north of the village. It is heavily shored and propped, but it probably looks better than it did a century ago when its trunk was a patchwork of iron and tin, the effort of villagers who thought they knew a thing or two about tree preservation.

The bole was hollowed out by a 19th century innkeeper and fitted with a circular table and seating for a dozen people. A door was fixed to the outside, and one exists to this day. On Palm Sundays in the old days there was always a fair around the much loved tree where 'ale flows free and mirth rises high'.

The tree and the churchyard have had rather a forlorn appearance of late, but it must have been much worse in the 17th century before, it was recorded, 'part of ye body of Crohurst Church, which had lien in heaps a long time, was made plain and repaired'. The church, which probably dates from the 12th century, has memorials to the Gainsfords and the Angells, at one time the two big families in the district.

🍁 DEEPCUT

This is one of several communities close to Camberley whose name will be familiar to generations of former national servicemen. More recently, in the late 1980s, the Alma Dettingen barracks were used as emergency prison accommodation. The barracks were converted in 33 days at a cost of £500,000 to house more than 330 specially selected category C prisoners. These were inmates serving time for minor offences, and it was part of Home Secretary Douglas Hurd's scheme to deal with prison overcrowding. In spite of the fact that the prisoners were low category, the Home Office still had 390 service personnel to guard them. The assistant governor, in an interview with a *Surrey Advertiser* reporter, said it was unlikely anyone would manage to escape. 'Even if they got over the razor wire, they would have to face the Gurkhas. After them we've got the RAF dog display team, and then there's the Royal Irish Rangers, to say nothing of the unexploded bomb sites!'

Although troop training continues on the neighbouring commons, the military presence in and around Deepcut is nowhere near what is was. The name is probably better known now when associated with the Basingstoke Canal which runs parallel to the mainline railway from London Waterloo to the South West.

🍁 DIPPENHALL

This collection of houses and farms to the north-west of Farnham is just in Surrey, and will always be associated with

Harold Falkner, the celebrated architect of Farnham. Falkner, with the assistance of two labourers, built nine houses at Dippenhall between 1921 and his death in 1963. One, Burles, comprises two barns brought from Gloucestershire and placed end to end.

Falkner, a contemporary of Lutyens and godson of Gertrude Jekyll, was a legend in his own lifetime, at least in Farnham. He was spoken of in hushed, reverential tones and, to me, as a junior reporter on the *Farnham Herald* in the early 1960s, he was a god-like figure. One hesitated to become involved in stories concerning Harold Falkner and it was, therefore, with some trepidation that I prepared for my first meeting with the great man. It must have been a year or so before the architect's death that my editor, the late Mr Theo Pope – a man whose feeling for the town of Farnham came through in every word he wrote – asked me to return some material to Mr Falkner, who lived in West Street and quite close to our offices. I was to knock and enter and proceed through to a back room where I would find the architect. It was a bright day but inside the house it was dark and cheerless. A voice, weak with old age, called out. I traced it to the appropriate room, which was darker still, and as I announced myself I was unsure of the man's whereabouts. I needed to remain in that room no longer than it took to state my business, and to this day I cannot say how he was positioned or indeed whether he was on a bed or a sofa.

The Falkner legend lives on in the town, where houses he ‘ designed are in much demand. There are good examples in the Great Austins area to the south of the railway line as well as in Dippenhall. This little corner of Surrey is largely unknown outside Farnham and district and, in spite of the increase in traffic which has turned the lanes into a perceived shortcut to and from the M3, it still has plenty of rural charm.

🍁 DITTON, THAMES

Thames Ditton has been described as 'an oasis of old world survival'. It is the place where Eros, the statue in London's Piccadilly Circus, had its birth, in a foundry in Summer Road. In the churchyard of St Nicholas is the gravestone of Lady Pamela Fitzgerald, known as 'La Belle Pamela'. Her father, the Duke of Orleans, was guillotined during the French Revolution, and her husband, Lord Edward Fitzgerald, was shot by the English. Lady Pamela's half-brother, Louis Phillipe, became King of France, and ended his days in exile at Claremont at Esher. She died in 1831 and was buried in Montmartre, but during the siege of Paris in 1870 a German shell wrecked her gravestone, and so her remains were brought to Thames Ditton. Another gravestone records the burial of Cuthbert Blakeden, 'Serjeant of the Confectionary to King Henry VIII'.

🍁 DOCKENFIELD

This hamlet is as far west as you can go in Surrey. The boundary with Hampshire meanders around it and often it is unclear just which county you are in. Dockenfield is hard by Alice Holt Forest which is over the border and was the home of Lord Baden-Powell, the founder of the Boy Scout movement. The village war memorial is unusual in that it has a pitched roof. Batts Corner, where a nonconformist chapel has been converted into a house, is on the road to Rowledge, and the Blue Bell pub has been a popular haunt over the years. It was once a bakery. The road to Frensham church passes Frensham mill, where the languid water of the river Wey is always a good place for a spot of bird-watching, while the road through

DORMANSLAND ▓ THE SURREY VILLAGE BOOK

Spreakley Hollow is where you can observe sand martins nesting in the cliffs above the river.

🍁 DORMANSLAND

A pleasant drive around the back of Lingfield racecourse brings you to Dormans railway station and then on to Dormansland. The station was opened in 1884 and was at first called Bellagio. Dormansland is a collection of cottages and houses along a main road but nearby are two important buildings. Greathed Manor was formerly Ford Manor and built in 1868 by Robert Kerr who wrote *The Gentleman's House*. Like so many of our larger old properties, Greathed is now used for commercial purposes. Old Surrey Hall is right on the county border with Sussex and very close to the boundary with Kent. It was built around 1450 and underwent restoration in the 1920s. 'Imitation carried to the point of genius,' said Pevsner and Nairn. They added: 'The architect must have been working quite cut off from reality, and his flair for detail carries the onlooker over into the fairytale world.'

🍁 DOWNSIDE

This is popular commuter country because of its closeness to the M25 and the railway. Downside is situated just inside the orbital motorway and linked to the 'world beyond' by the road to Effingham Junction station. Its proximity to Cobham and Esher makes it popular with people wishing to move out of London but not as far as, say, Guildford.

🍁 DUNSFOLD

As at Crowhurst, a much loved yew tree stands beside the church of St Mary and All Saints in Dunsfold. The churchyard is perfect peace, separated from the village by fields and woods. Peace, that is, when the jets are not flying low over the countryside from the nearby airfield. Until it underwent a name change and then closure, one of the pubs in the village was called the Hawk and Harrier, which served as a constant reminder of the importance to British aviation that is attached to the aerodrome that takes its name from this sleepy village.

But back to the yew tree which is reputed to be 1,000 years old. It certainly looks it, standing there by virtue of a multitude of props and wires. The setting of the church is completely rural, but so is the village. Dunsfold is off the beaten track and therefore largely unspoilt. Eric Parker wrote long ago of a Dunsfold lane ... 'a wild plum tree branching out of a hedge dressed with the whitest of delicate blossom, and in the white blossom, with the hot blue of a May sky beyond and between, a nightingale's throat throbbing with singing.' Those Dunsfold lanes still exist to delight the visitor; the nightingales may be harder to find.

In the reign of Elizabeth I the lanes would have resounded to the gossip of the locals when, in the fortnight before Christmas 1578, Thomas Mellersh was stabbed to death. His brother Harvey, a Dunsfold yeoman, was found guilty of the crime at Pond Close and sentenced to hang. Their sister Elizabeth and Elizabeth Burle, a servant of their father, were found guilty of being accessories. History does not record the motive.

Gertrude Jekyll, that great observer of the countryside in South West Surrey, recorded a saying that was frequently heard in the district when praise was being accorded a man who was wide awake or more than ordinarily intelligent. 'He's got his head screwed on the right way', ran the line which now has a more widespread use.

🍁 EASHING

This sleepy hollow off the A3, through which the Wey meanders, was for centuries an important river crossing. The Romans knew it as they marched from the Weald to Wansdyke, a great fortification from Berkshire to the Bristol Channel. The bridge at Eashing, with seven arches, was built in the 13th century, almost without doubt by the monks from Waverley Abbey. The National Trust owns the bridge and the cottages near it, the latter bought for £400 in 1902.

A modern bridge takes the Godalming and Guildford bypass over the river a quarter of a mile above Eashing where, during construction of the original bypass road, skeletons were found. A Roman hairpin was lying near to the head of one of those buried who were thought to have died in times of peace.

There has been a mill at Eashing probably since the time of Domesday. Although Eashing was not named in the survey, Peper Harow was and it lies just across the main road. It seems likely that the mill at Pipereherge (valued at 15s in 1086) was on the site of the building that has been at Eashing throughout the 20th century and which has undergone much change as a small business park is developed beside the river.

A chapel, long since disused, has been removed from Eashing and is now one the many attractions at the Rural Life Museum between Tilford and Frensham.

🍁 EFFINGHAM

Howard of Effingham School and the Lord Howard pub are reminders of the connection the great seafaring Howards had with this village between Guildford and Leatherhead. It was Lord Charles Howard, the second earl, who was most famous, for he was commander-in-chief of the fleet aboard *Ark Royal* against the Spanish Armada. His leadership brought victory and the title of the Earl of Nottingham in 1588.

Lord Charles's father, Lord William of Effingham, beat the Scots at Flodden Field. He was the son of the second Duke of Norfolk, and was granted Reigate Priory which had been built in the early 13th century for Augustinian canons. Effingham was sold by the third Earl of Howard in 1647.

Effingham today is a convenient place in which to live: handy shops, attractive houses, golf course, quick access to beautiful countryside, and, close by, a railway station on a loop line to London. The church is dedicated to St Lawrence, and Aubrey noted in 1718 a small fair on the feast of the saint (August 10), but this event has long been abandoned.

A property in Lower Road is a Lutyens design and said to be one of the finest early houses from the Surrey architect. Recently in use as a convent, it was originally known as Red House and had a garden by that great Lutyens collaborator Gertrude Jekyll.

🍁 EGHAM

North of the bypass of this town is Runnymede, 182 acres of meadows which has given its name to the local council. Two important monuments draw tourists from all corners of the world. The Magna Carta was signed here in 1215 and is

Magna Carta Memorial,
Runnymede, Surrey.
G. Hawkins

remembered by a memorial designed by Sir Edward Maufe, the architect of Guildford Cathedral, and unveiled in 1957. It was in the Runnymede meadows that the all powerful King John, while staying at Windsor Castle, accepted the demands of his barons and signed the document that bestowed liberty and freedom on the country. On the slopes above is the Kennedy Memorial which was paid for by public subscription and unveiled by the Queen in 1965. The assassination of John F. Kennedy in Dallas in 1964 was one of those world events that will forever be remembered. The question, 'Where were you at the time?' will have been asked over and over again by visitors to Runnymede.

The Egham races were held in the riverside meadows during the 18th and 19th centuries. They were cancelled, and not revived, in 1886 when the police refused to provide officers to keep law and order at the track.

🍁 ELSTEAD

It is likely the mill on the Wey was one of the six unnamed Farnham mills recorded in the Domesday Book, but no one can be sure. How many times has it been stated categorically that Elstead and its mill appeared in the survey of 1086? The mill is now a restaurant; at the end of the 19th century it was a worsted factory employing 55 people. Since then, with its manufacturing life at an end, the mill house has had a variety of occupants, including the village policeman; a motoring pioneer, Mr Chaplin Court Treatt, who drove from the Cape to Cairo across the Sahara, and was given a tremendous homecoming with the village band at the head of the procession; and one of the brothers Bentley of motor car fame.

The present mill is not the original building; that burnt down in the 17th century soon after Cromwell's troops had occupied it during the Civil War. Nearby, the refurbished bridge over the river Wey has sections up to 700 years old but, sadly, its glory is partly hidden by the functional though ugly modern crossing which carries traffic into the village.

Elstead green has always been the focal point of the village, and around it stand some notable buildings, including Springfield Farm and the Woolpack. Between the green and the river is the Golden Fleece, another public house whose name recalls the days when Elstead's income came from wool.

The commons around the village have long been favoured for military training purposes, and during the wars were centres for billeting the troops. George V visited the soldiers during

The church at Elstead.

the First World War, leaving his car by St James's church and riding his horse down Westbrook Hill and on to Hankley Common. Lord Kitchener also reviewed the men but, in a *Farnham Herald* article in 1981, it was recalled that difficulties in lowering a flag were considered a bad omen. Soon afterwards Kitchener, the Secretary of State for War, lost his life at sea when on a visit to Russia.

Waverley Abbey's foundation charter in 1128 was the first time in which Elstead was named. Calling it Helestede, the abbey's founder, Bishop William Giffard, gave the Cistercian order near Farnham two acres of land. The church of St James was built about 1138 and served by the priests of Waverley. When the abbey was dissolved in 1536 Elstead, with Seale and Frensham became chapelries of Farnham. The first resident priest came to the village in 1829, but for much of the remainder of the 19th century the rector was a Yorkshireman, Joseph Rhodes Charlesworth, who, when he died in 1904, had completed 50 years as the incumbent. He was buried in the churchyard where a Cedar of Lebanon had been planted in 1849 as a thanks offering for relief from cholera which had spread death throughout the village.

There is a fine Lutyens house, Fulbrook, on the road to Cutt Mill, built in 1896 as a wedding present for Mr and Mrs Gerard Streatfeild. The builder was Andrew Chuter, of Frensham, who had built Pierrepont in his home village to the design of Norman Shaw. Mrs Streatfeild was the daughter of Richard Combe of Pierrepont, and she worked with Gertrude Jekyll on the first garden. Her chauffeur was this writer's grandfather who had learned to drive in Hyde Park and, he always claimed, had been the first person to hold a driving licence in Surrey. Grandfather, who was 'volunteered' by his employers to drive a London bus in the capital during the General Strike, lived in the lodge at Fulbrook which, say Pevsner and Nairn, is 'another stroke of genius on a tiny scale. One gable and a very tall bold chimneystack ...' My late father was born in the lodge and as a boy knew the cottage below the big house as a laundry. It is now a private house and has been owned during the last 35 years by, among others, the late Peter Sellers and the Beatles drummer Ringo Starr. My days as a junior reporter on the

Farnham Herald took me to Brookfield on the day Peter Sellers married the then little known actress Britt Ekland. The media jostled on the lawn as Sellers, in his best Goon voice, dominated a very public reception with a somewhat bemused Britt by his side. Sellers and Britt became popular figures in the village – often seen on bicycles when he was recuperating from his first much publicised heart attack.

ENGLEFIELD GREEN

This large village out towards Berkshire has on its outskirts the 'most ebullient Victorian building in the Home Counties', according to Pevsner and Nairn. Royal Holloway College on the A30 was built by W.H. Crossland in 1879-87 for Thomas Holloway. It was one of the first colleges for women (Girton was already open) and was the twin of Holloway Sanitorium at nearby Virginia Water. Crossland was a pupil of Sir George Gilbert Scott, who designed much in Surrey in the 19th century. Holloway made his fortune from the worldwide sale of Holloway's Pills. The college measures 550ft by 376ft and is built around a double courtyard in the French Renaissance style. It became part of the University of London in 1900 and has admitted male students since 1965.

'Though deep, yet clear-though gentle yet not dull;
Strong without rage; without o'erflowing full'

Those lines by Sir John Denham in 1643 were inspired by the view from Coopers Hill to the north of Englefield Green. The view is of Runnymede and the Thames and in addition to a large training college there is the Commonwealth Air Forces Memorial which was erected by the Commonwealth War Graves Commission. It commemorates the Commonwealth air force personnel who lost their lives in the Second World War. When the Queen unveiled the memorial in 1953 there were more than 25,000 relatives of the dead airmen present. On the slopes of Coopers Hill is the Kennedy Memorial and at the foot the Magna Carta Memorial.

🍁 ESHER

A town with a village feel. The two big attractions which bring thousands of people to Esher are Claremont and Sandown Park racecourse. Lord Clive had Lancelot 'Capability' Brown and Henry Holland build the present Claremont in 1768, spending £100,000 on the house and gardens after pulling down the original property which had been erected by Sir John Vanbrugh in 1708 in the reign of Queen Anne. Vanbrugh called it 'Romantick' and sold it to the Earl of Clare (later the Duke of Newcastle). By a special Act of Parliament in 1816 it was purchased as a residence for Princess Charlotte on the occasion of her marriage to Prince Leopold. When she died Leopold continued to live there until he was elected King of the Belgians. Queen Victoria, who was Leopold's niece, spent much of her childhood at Claremont and the property eventually passed to her. The monarch gave it to her youngest son, the Duke of Albany, and from there things became complicated because of the royal household's foot in both camps at the outbreak of the First World War. Eventually, Claremont was sold at auction and today it is one of Surrey's most visited estates.

Sandown Park racecourse has also had its share of royal patronage since it was established in 1875 on the site of one of Esher's three historic manors which was called Sandon. A 12th century church hospital had been situated there and this had merged with St Thomas's in London in the 15th century before being confiscated by the Crown.

🍁 EWHURST

A Roman villa at Rapsley to the north of this village was discovered in 1956. Its date of occupancy has been put at AD 80-
350 and the inhabitants probably made tiles and raised stock.
The villa was unearthed when Hareholt Copse was being
replanted, and archaeologists completed the work in 1968.
Evidence of a Roman road through the parish has been proved
as an offshoot of Stone or Stane Street.

The windmill at Ewhurst was, at 800ft above sea level, a
notable landmark, but it ceased work in 1885 and was converted into a house around the turn of the century.

The church of St Peter and St Paul was mostly rebuilt after
'tinkering repairs' to the ancient central part of the tower and
its wooden steeple brought the lot crashing down in 1839.

North-west of the village is the Hurtwood; high, wooded
ground with some fine houses, one of which, Long Copse, was
considered by G.F. Watts, the Victorian painter who lived at
Compton, to be the most beautiful in Surrey.

Between Ewhurst and Walliswood is dinosaur country –
well, the remains of the prehistoric beasts. At the Smokejacks
brickworks, the bones of a number of dinosaurs have been discovered over the years, the most significant being the remains
of *Baryonyx Walkeri*, a near-complete 10-metre-long fish-eat-
ing specimen found by an amateur fossil collector in 1983. It
is now on display in the Natural History Museum in London.

🍁 FAIRLANDS

There is a strong sense of community at this housing development within the parish of Worplesdon. It is situated off the
Aldershot road between Guildford and Normandy, and not far

from Merrist Wood College, where agricultural students from around the world have studied over the years. The college has had to keep abreast of the times, particularly financially, and has given over some of its land to a golf course, one of many to be developed around Guildford during an increase in the game's popularity in the last ten years. In fact, as farmland became redundant and farmers saw the prospect of a good financial return, there were so many plans for new courses that, taken together with the clubs already established, it was once said, lightheartedly, that it might be possible to hit a golf ball from course to course around the Borough of Guildford.

During the Second World War, a Halifax bomber returning from a mission was brought down by 'friendly' fire and crashed into a field at Merrist Wood. Its remains were unearthed in 1997 and, through diligent and thorough research, a local aviation historian has written an absorbing book about F-Freddie and the men who were on that ill-fated flight.

🍁 Farleigh

On the map the boundary with Greater London forms an umbrella above Farleigh up in the north-east corner of the county. It is drawn in that fashion thanks to the fighting qualities of the local residents, for Farleigh was intended to be included in the London Borough of Croydon when the local government boundaries were changed in the 1970s.

In 1908 Farley, as it was then spelt, caught Eric Parker's attention. He wrote of the tiny church by a fine farmyard where all was not well, in his opinion. 'Its modest spire, as you walk to the churchyard, is dominated and affronted by the hideous clock tower of a neighbouring lunatic asylum. Why should such a thing be?' he asked. 'County councils have decreed that in this part of Surrey must be massed together the

thousands of poor souls who have lost the reason which county councillors must be supposed to possess; but why insist on
their unhappy presence? A building to hold such sadness
should be a quiet thing, hidden among trees, silent, alone. But
that would suit neither councillors nor architects. For them,
asylums must stare, scar, insist that they will be seen and
known; and here, in what should be tranquil and lovely country, they violate the hills!'

🍁 FARLEY GREEN

Those two great writers on Surrey, Aubrey and Bray, brought
this area to the notice of a wider audience in 1672 and 1803
respectively, but it was not until Martin Tupper discovered the
'Roman Temple' on Farley Heath that one of the south's finest
Romano-British camps was determined. Farley Heath was
known as 'Little Surrey Pompeii' when Tupper, between 1839
and 1847, spent 'random hours grubbing' with encouraging
but inconclusive results.

Then, between February and July 1848, he supervised
three men, from the nearby estate of the Duke of
Northumberland, who worked continuously and made many
interesting discoveries. An Albury schoolmaster, Mr Lovell,
'grubbed' in December 1852 and found British coins and a
horse's bit, and much later, in 1926, Mr S.E. Winbolt dug there
and found pottery.

The importance of the camp at Farley Heath, which had
been known as Old Bury, hence the name Albury, kept the
archaeologists busy, and further digging in 1939 was interrupted by the start of the war. Many of the discoveries made to
that date are on display in Guildford Museum.

The first proper excavation was carried in 1995 after
English Heritage had approached Surrey County Council. In a

dig lasting ten weeks, archaeologists mapped out a ground plan of the temple, and subsequently provided an information panel with an artist's impression of the site as it might have looked almost 2,000 years ago.

Nonconformist worship in Farley Green dates back to 1888, and its origins are simple. The story goes that a Gomshall man, Mr Abel Overington, and his two sons walked the three miles to Farley Green one Sunday afternoon in an attempt to interest the people in a spot of preaching and hymn singing. When the visitors arrived they found everyone out on the green, but it was not a welcoming party. The men and boys were playing cricket, while the womenfolk were watching. Typical of many a village green in high summer.

Mr Overington was undaunted. He told the people of his intent and several joined him for an open-air service in one corner of the green. One of his boys led the singing on his flute, and a resident brought chairs from her cottage. The gathering was such a success that Mr Overington returned the following week and for the next two summers. Then a cottage was offered for winter services, and eventually, with the pioneering Mr Overington moving on, the congregation came more under the wing of the chapel in Gomshall.

🍁 FARNCOMBE

This urban village between Godalming and Guildford was recorded in the Domesday Book as being held by the Bishop of Bayeux. It is separated from its bigger neighbour by the Lammas Lands, riverside meadows where for centuries cattle have grazed.

Farncombe was the birthplace of one of the heroes of the *Titanic*, the ill-fated liner which struck an iceberg and sank on its maiden Atlantic voyage in April 1912. Jack George Phillips was the chief wireless operator on the ship and by remaining at his post he sacrificed his life. In Godalming, the Phillips Memorial Garden, designed by Thackeray Turner and laid out by Gertrude Jekyll, is an everlasting reminder of this brave man. There is also a memorial to him in Farncombe's St John the Evangelist church where he was a choirboy.

The church was built in 1847 and, according to the *Surrey Advertiser* in 1922, stands on what was known as the 'Field of Blood' because it was the site of the execution in 1840 of a youth who had poisoned his uncle.

Red-bricked almshouses alongside the main road were built in 1622 by Richard Wyatt, a wealthy benefactor who lived at Hall Place, Shackleford. Wyatt was the Master of the Worshipful Company of Carpenters and laid down that an 'Oyspitall' be built for 'tenn poore men'. The City livery company's officers continue to make regular visits to the almshouses.

Almost opposite the almshouses are extensive playing fields where once stood Broadwater House, home of the Marshalls, and renowned for its cricketing links. There was a fine ground at the house on which many of the great 19th and early 20th century players performed. The Marshall brothers, the Hon Alexander and the Hon Frederick, were prominent members of the local cricket scene in the middle and second half of the 19th century, and their hospitality was well known. In 1852 an England XI played there and the great player of an earlier age, William 'Silver Billy' Beldham, then aged 86, walked the seven miles from his home at Tilford to watch the game. He was described as possessing 'a perfectly upright bearing, looked to be about 70 years old, used a stick in walking, and had a profusion of white silvery hair of considerable length, dropping down to his shoulders. His complexion was remarkably fresh and ruddy and, notwithstanding his great age, he was even then a splendid specimen of a veteran athlete.'

Unitarian Chapel, Meadrow, Farncombe. L Howkins

Beldham and his friends and acquaintances would be delighted that a range of sports, including cricket, football, rugby, golf and tennis, continues to be played and enjoyed on and about that spot.

Broadwater Lake is popular with anglers who ring its banks and frequently catch some of the big specimens that lurk in its depths.

Indeed, for many years, Broadwater appeared in the list of record catches for freshwater fish in this country.

🍁 FELBRIDGE

The Evelyn family have roots in this settlement hard against the Sussex border and on the north-western outskirts of East Grinstead. They lived at Felbridge Place and would have been involved in the formation of a separate ecclesiastical parish at the time St John the Divine church was built in 1865. The Weald iron industry was strong in this area and mill ponds are a reminder of that age.

🍁 FETCHAM

A book published in the 1940s said of Fetcham that it was 'rapidly filling up'. Well, in the subsequent half a century it achieved its quota and some would say spilled over. Fetcham can hardly be classed as a village now; more a suburb of Leatherhead and a continuation of Great Bookham. In days gone by though it was divorced from its neighbour and as rural as the next village. The river Mole has played a large part in the life of the community and its presence still forms an effective boundary between Fetcham and Leatherhead.

At the time of Domesday Fetcham boasted five mills, had a

one-sixth share in another and a one-third stake in a seventh. Part of St Mary's church may be pre-Conquest, and a Saxon cemetery was discovered during building work in the neighbourhood. Another venerable building is the Old Rising Sun restaurant which has a 1348 date linked to it but is more likely to be 15th century. For years it was an ale house and beer was brewed on the premises using local hops. That was an industry to be found throughout Surrey, for in addition to the acres of hop fields there were small areas of bines which were grown to produce local beers. The custom returned in the latter of part of the 20th century with the upsurge in interest and support for real ale.

Among those buried in the churchyard are Admiral Sir George Henry Richardson, who was well known as a hydrographer and expert in submarine telegraphy, and Sir Francis Graham Moon, who was a printer and publisher and Lord Mayor of London in 1854. His eldest son, Sir Edward Graham Moon, was rector of Fetcham from 1859 until his death in 1904.

The mill pond at Fetcham caught Eric Parker's imagination. It was 'unlike any other pond I know. It is two or three hundred yards long and perhaps eighty yards wide, slopes gradually from the sides over a chalky bottom, and is of an intense clear green.' He was fascinated by the 'uncanny motion' of the water. The springs have since been harnessed by a water company and are now under manholes but visible to anyone who cares to ask the right question.

🍁 FOREST GREEN

Open-air services with the preacher using a farm wagon as a pulpit were a common sight around these parts a century or so ago. The Sunday afternoon missionaries used to thump out the message as the tide of nonconformism swept over the southern part of the county. In June 1878, though, steps were taken to build a chapel, and Master John Evelyn, son of the lord of the manor, was led along by his nurse to lay a memorial stone. Soon the building was ready for use and the faithful had a permanent home for their services.

The present Holy Trinity church is tucked away off the Ewhurst road and when it was dedicated on 30 January 1897, it replaced the St Barnabas Mission Room which had been built 10 years earlier. The church was erected as a memorial to their eldest son, Ernest Charles Everard, by Charles Ernest and Emily Christina Hensley, of Pratsham Grange. The main gates were the gift of the people of the village in 1945 as a thanskgiving for peace.

The original village hall was built in 1920 and destroyed by fire on 4 February 1954. More than three and a half years later a clubroom was provided and then, on 20 February 1988, the present hall was opened. These facts are recorded on two plaques attached to the building. The first building was erected through the influence and support of Mr and Mrs Lawrence Briant, of Forest Green House, aided by their many friends. It was opened on 13 November 1920 by Princess Helena Victoria CBE. The plaque goes on to state that the structure, together with much equipment, was presented by the YMCA for the promotion of the objects by which the Forest Green Red Triangle Club was established. These included the encouragement and development of the highest ends of the body, mind and spirit of the young life of the community. The hall was to provide a common meeting place, both inter-denominational and non-political, to offer facilities for recreation, intellectual improvement and character formation in a healthy, social, civic and Christian atmosphere. A seat of remembrance and shelter to the memory of Lawrence Briant JP, who spent his life in the service of others, was erected in 1925 by his friend and helper Frederick Higgs.

The cricket club, established in 1895, has been on its present ground opposite the village hall and the Parrot Inn, with Leith Hill as a backdrop, since the 1920s.

There was a track from Forest Green over the back of Leith Hill which was known as Smugglers' Way, and contraband aplenty was shipped towards the capital through the thickly wooded countryside. The Oke stream springs up at Pitland Street on the eastern slope of Holmbury Hill and at High Ashes on the western slope of Leith Hill and flows past Forest Green and nearby Oakwoodhill to meet other tributaries and form the north branch of the Arun in Sussex.

🍁 FRENSHAM

Everyone's heard of Frensham Pond. At least it seems like it on a summer's day when the sand beside this large expanse of water resembles Brighton on a bank holiday. Few of the visitors, though, will know of the pond's and the district's history.

Frensham Great Pond, to give it its correct name, and to distinguish it from its smaller neighbour, was noted as early as 1208 when it belonged to the Bishop of Winchester and provided him with fish for his table in Farnham Castle. Almost two miles in circumference, it covers the site of a natural pool which was subsequently enlarged. Bowen's map of 1749 recorded that Frensham had 'springs not inferior to those of Tunbridge Wells'.

The first seaplane was tested on the pond in 1913 and while that was a happy and successful occasion there have been many sad times, fortunately not recently, when bathers have drowned. Local children always had the dangers of the pond spelt out, such as its varying depth close into the shore and its hidden weed. But visitors were often not so well informed and all too often tragedy ended a day out in the country.

Frensham Great Pond
from The King's Ridge

Across the main road and over King's Ridge lies the Little Pond which was formed in 1246. It, too, provided fish for the bishops, while a third and now almost unknown mere called Abbot's Pond at nearby Tilford was created to supply the monks of Waverley Abbey. The dam of that pond burst in 1841 and was never restored; the stream being dammed lower down to create the present Stockbridge Pond, a tranquil spot known to anglers and walkers.

During the Second World War both ponds at Frensham were drained to prevent them being used as directional aids to enemy bombers as they lined up for raids on military targets at Aldershot and Bordon.

The parish of Frensham is far-flung but small when compared with former days when it not only included Churt, as it continues to do, but Hindhead and Shottermill as well. Millbridge crossroads have never aligned and for years there was a white stone on the roadside which caught out many a motorist. It was originally placed there when the Farnham to Hindhead road was made and was intended to keep heavy wagons and their loads from bumping into the house on the corner.

Pierrepont, a school until it became the base of a Christian ministry a few years ago, was a private house before the Second World War, owned by the Combe family who were members of the Watney brewing concern. The last lady of the house was a Lady in her own right and went to extraordinary lengths to let people know. She was The Lady Constance Combe and many a soul committed the unforgivable sin of omitting the definite article. Tradesmen were even sent back from whence they had come if the parcel they bore did not include that three letter word.

St Mary's is old but little remains of the church first built on the site in 1239. It is situated above the river Wey and close to some lovely old cottages. A large cauldron in the church has confounded people for centuries. Did it belong to Mother Ludlam, the Waverley witch? Or was it once in the kitchen of Waverley Abbey? We will probably never know.

🍁 FRIDAY STREET

'You turn a corner of the road and you are in Switzerland', said Eric Parker, rather extravagantly, of Friday Street. It is indeed a beautiful place with a pond, some cottages and an inn. In pre-motor car days it was probably more romantic with the smell of wood smoke filling the valley. The pond can probably be dated to the time of Domesday, and the miller ground corn. Later iron, wire and gunpowder were made in this quiet spot. The powder mill was established during the reign of Henry VIII and was said to be the first of its kind in England. Rocque's map of 1762 recorded a mill pond but not a mill.

The inn is named after Stephen Langton, the Archbishop of Canterbury in King John's time, whose image is depicted in a set of small carved heads above the south door of Wotton church.

🍁 FRIMLEY

Ethel Smyth, a celebrated composer and pianist, who died in 1944, went to Frimley school after moving to the village in 1867, at the age of nine, when her father took a command at nearby Aldershot.

It would have been a small place in those days. Nowadays it is part of a conurbation that continues to grow with the economic boom in the Blackwater Valley, whose eponymous Road has opened up the area between the A31 Hog's Back and the M3. Frimley is at the northern end of the BVR, and through traffic need not know that there is still a heart of 'old' Frimley which is a busy little centre but still identifiable. The county boundary follows the meandering river Blackwater and anything east of it is in Surrey.

The conurbation mentioned above tends to be largely in Hampshire and stretches from Aldershot through Farnborough to Camberley, which is in Surrey but close to both Hampshire and Berkshire.

The main hospital for this densely populated area is Frimley Park, and it has taken on an increasing workload since the closure of the Cambridge Military Hospital at Aldershot.

Anything at Camberley that resembled a village disappeared a long time ago. However, in days gone by when the military was becoming established there was a village atmosphere. The Royal Military College was moved to Sandhurst, which is now in Berkshire, in 1809 and York Town took shape. The name came from the Duke of York of nursery rhyme fame. The Staff College was built in 1862 and, it is said, Prince Albert caught his fatal chill watching its construction.

❧ FRIMLEY GREEN

This bustling area is a far cry from the days when there was more heather than houses. The heaths are still there but at arm's length. It is now firmly commuter land. There are no highwaymen on the barren heaths and no caves in the sand where the booty was hidden. It was a place with a gibbet but the last public execution was in 1850 when three men were hanged for the murder of the parish priest in the parsonage – which was said to be haunted for years after.

The railway and the canal opened up the district, but the two did not always go together. Once, the aqueduct carrying the canal over the railway sprung a leak and had to be closed because the escaping water was damping the fires in the engines passing underneath. The Basingstoke Canal was cut through Frimley Green upon the conclusion of the War of Independence, although the work had been authorised by an Act of Parliament in 1778. Ten years later a private company using Irish labour began the work and the canal was opened in 1796. Of its original 37 miles from Basingstoke to the river Wey at Weybridge, 32 miles have been restored and were opened for recreational use by the Duke of Kent in 1991. The 15-mile stretch from the Wey to the Hampshire border rises 195ft through 28 locks. Road and rail transport had put paid

to the canal as a profitable means of shifting cargo, and it fell
into disrepair.

🍁 GATTON

You will not find a village here but it is a place with a good deal
of history attached to it. It once returned two members to
Parliament and earned the wrath of Cobbett who called it a
'very rascally spot of earth'. It was a Rotten Borough but the
Reform Act of 1832 put a stop to all that, and upset the plans
of the new owner, Lord Monson, who, only two years earlier,
had paid £100,000 for the estate and the power that went
with it.

The Domesday Book recorded a church at Gatton, but the

present one, dedicated to St Andrew, is 13th century. Lord Monson, who was the fifth baron, filled it with treasures from Europe during the 1830s. In the park is what has been called the smallest town hall in Britain, built in the form of a portico in 1765 and from which Gatton's owner sent the two MPs to Westminster.

Monson's mansion was burnt down in the 1930s but not before Sir Jeremiah Colman, of mustard fame, had been an owner. Today, Gatton is popular with walkers following the North Downs Way, and the old park has been bisected by the M25.

🍁 GODSTONE

Cobbett took this village to his heart but he would surely shudder today. He found peace and quiet in the White Hart which is still a comfortable inn overlooking the green but too close to a busy road junction for comfort. Godstone is on the A25 and has a raceway of a one-way traffic system around its centre where the A22 comes in from the south.

'Godstone', wrote Cobbett in 1822, 'is a beautiful village, chiefly of one street with a fine large green before it and with a pond in the green. A little way to the right (going from London) lies the vile Rotten Borough of Bletchingley, but, happily for Godstone, out of sight. At and near Godstone the gardens are all very neat and, at the inn, there is a nice garden well stocked with beautiful flowers in the season. I saw here, last summer, some double violets as large as small pinks, and the lady of the house was kind enough to give me some roots.'

The march of time has changed Godstone. But the gardens are still pretty and the green and the pond are still opposite the inn. The White Hart was probably built in the reign of Edward II and altered in the Elizabethan period. At one time it was known as the Clayton Arms after Sir Robert Clayton, the son of a carpenter from Northamptonshire. Clayton made his money as a scrivener and became Lord Mayor of London. By the time he died in 1707 he was the biggest landowner in the district of Godstone and Bletchingley in whose church there is a memorial.

Godstone in very recent times has been pinpointed as one of several locations in the county where good quantities of oil are thought to be beneath the surface. Four hundred years ago it was the centre of the Surrey leather trade. Godstone, it seems, has always been a busy centre, and one which needed to rebuild after being devastated by the Black Death.

The appropriately named Walker Miles, who was a pioneer of rambling clubs, is buried at Godstone, whose church dedicated to St Nicholas was restored in 1872 by Sir George Gilbert Scott who lived at Rooks Nest nearby. Scott was also responsible for St Mary's almshouses to the south of the church.

Walker Miles was the *nom de plume* of Edmund Seyfang Taylor (1853-1908), who became known as the Chief Path Finder and wrote books of routes for ramblers. A sarsen stone in the churchyard records that it was erected by members of the rambling clubs of London 'who knew the man and admired his works'. Miles was to Surrey what Wainwright has become in the Lake District and the Pennines around a century later. The main difference between the two is one of communication. Whereas Miles was able to get his message across in a parochial way, the late A. Wainwright, for all his efforts to remain reclusive, has become, through mass communication and multi-media techniques, something of a cult figure upon whose back there is considerable money to be made.

Two yeoman from the village were hanged in Elizabethan times for attacking one Michael Knight in the highway. Lewis Hobbye and Matthew Bone were the defendants and Hobbye was said to have thrust at Knight with a staff and inflicted injuries from which he died the following day. A jury found them guilty on 10 November 1582.

🍁 GOMSHALL

Tanneries, which closed in 1988, once dominated this small village on the A25. Rebuilt and expanded after a fire in 1890, they were known to visitors from around the world. Now the site is to be developed with houses. The former Black Horse, now a restaurant, was probably a malthouse at the end of the 17th century and was a brewery into the 20th century. The Compasses was built in 1830 and was originally a beer shop, transferring to an inn around 1886. King John House on the corner of Queen Street and the main road was built, according to local legend, shortly after the plague in 1666 on the profits of hides collected in London.

The village was Gomeselle in the Domesday Book when there was a mill, but not the mill building of today. Gomshall was in the Blackheath Hundred and in 1086 there was land for 20 ploughs, 30 villagers and eight smallholders with 18 ploughs, and six slaves. The mill was valued at 40d, there were three acres of meadow and woodland with 30 pigs. The survey pointed out that 'the villagers of this village are exempt from all the Sheriff's concerns'. It added that the Bishop of Bayeux wrongfully placed half a hide of land of the manor in the manor of Bramley, and held it. It was in Gomshall before and after 1066. And in neighbouring Wotton Hundred the King had a hide in lordship which 'lies in the lands of Gomshall'.

🍁 GRAFHAM

Along the A281 are fine examples of old West Surrey cottages at Birtley Green and the hamlet of Grafham whose ecclesiastical district was formed in 1863 out of the civil parishes of Bramley and Dunsfold. The church of St Andrew at Grafham was built in 1861, designed and paid for by Henry Woodyer who lived at Grafham Grange. Woodyer, who died on 10 August 1896, and was buried in the churchyard, also designed St Peter's at Hascombe and was responsible for some interior alterations to Holy Trinity, the former cathedral church at the top of Guildford High Street. The son of Caleb Woodyer, a Guildford surgeon-doctor, his architecture can also be seen in several schools in Surrey, and in churches in Berkshire, Gloucestershire, Gwent, Herefordshire, Hertfordshire, Staffordshire and Yorkshire.

🍁 GRAYSWOOD

The people of Grayswood gathered almost as one against the coming of the oil men in the 1980s. Seismic tests concluded that substantial deposits of gas were contained deep in the sub-strata, and there was talk of Holmen's Grove becoming the biggest onshore gas field in the country. It all came to nought, though, after exploratory drilling, but the locals now have a deeper respect for their environment. The site pinpointed was in a valley north of Grayswood on the A286 where All Saints' church looks out on to the cricket green where a new pavilion and village hall is testimony to the good that can be achieved by the National Lottery.

Prestwick Lane, which runs away to Chiddingfold, is thought to be a modern corruption of Priest's Way.

Grayswood was part of Witley ecclesiastical parish up to the beginning of the 20th century when, through the generosity of a local man, Mr Alfred Hugh Harman, a church and vicarage were built. An architect from nearby Haslemere, Mr Axel Haig, drew up the plans and work began in February 1901. A year later the church was consecrated. Mr Harman, who lived at Grayswood Place, is remembered by a memorial tablet in the church, while both he and his wife are buried in the churchyard where there is an impressive memorial stone.

Local men who lost their lives in the wars are recalled on a memorial beside the road to Haslemere and which looks over a valley towards Hurthill and Gibbet Hill at Hindhead. It is a beautiful spot and I am forever reminded of an old country-man's saying about it, when talking about thunderstorms. In his rustic accent, he said: 'When thaat thunder gets stuck in thaat vaalley it don't come out too easy.'

The road to Haslemere climbs steadily from the Wheatsheaf public house. It is thought to have been made in 1757 and not so long ago was quite a test for motor vehicles. Nowadays, drivers hardly notice an incline, unless they get held up by a slow-moving heavy vehicle. Nearer Haslemere, Jesses was the home of the musician and instrument maker, Carl Dolmetsch, whose name, in classical music circles, is synonymous with the town.

🍁 HALE

Heavy traffic rumbles through this hillside village to the north of Farnham and takes away much of the natural charm. This state of affairs has been the topic of conversation for generations. Hale people have always been a tough breed and weathered every storm, but the 18th and 19th century buildings are suffering under the strain, and there is rightly concern being expressed. One building still going strong is the Bethel Chapel in Bethel Lane which celebrated its 150th anniversary in 1984. It was built in 1834 on a site where preachers had long attracted crowds to their open air services, and the opening ceremony hymn was specially written by the man who was to become the first headmaster of Hale school.

A public house that overlooked the recreation ground was taken over during the Second World War and never again was a pint served there. It was known as the Sir Colin Campbell and was home to the Hale Brass Band. Then, with the outbreak of war, it became a rescue depot and the men on duty slept on bunks in the former cellar, and often shared their vigil with Canadian soldiers who were stationed in the area. Hale has always played a major part in the story of brewing in the Farnham district, and when The British Grenadier disappeared in 1900 it was probably one of a score of houses which lost their licences in a magisterial crackdown, brought about, it was suggested, when one member of the bench joined the temperance movement.

Modern Hale is dominated by a large housing development at the top of the hill, but the heart is still around the recreation ground which borders the main road. There, the competitive Hale sportsmen have been tough opponents over the years at both football and cricket. 'The men from the hill' as they were dubbed at the turn of the century.

One of their best cricketers then was the vicar, the Rev George Edward Hitchcock, who devoted himself to the life of the parish for 16 years from 1894. Another fine batsman from these parts was Albert Baker who was good enough to have several seasons for Surrey and be the opening partner of both Tom Hayward and the legendary Jack Hobbs in the county championship in the early part of the 20th century.

When the Great War broke out in August 1914 it was to the door of Hale Institute that a notice was pinned which read: 'It is supposed the Farnham Ramblers were engaged with the Germans, which is more important than cricket.' The Ramblers were a team of businessmen who played in Farnham Park and sometimes at Hale, whose ground is just outside the boundary of the park, a wide expanse on the slopes above Farnham. Once the property of the Bishops of Winchester who lived in Farnham Castle, it is now controlled by Waverley Council. A popular walk from Hale crosses the park to emerge at the stile and alley described by George Sturt in his autobiographical *A Small Boy in the Sixties*.

Sturt (1863-1927), who used the pen-name George Bourne, called it The Stile. This is what he wrote: 'Three other stiles there were indeed – one at each of the other three corners of the Park, to say nothing of the one near The Pound up beyond the Castle; but these we seldom saw – they must have been half to three-quarters of a mile away if not more. The others moreover did not matter to us. Our stile – The Stile par excellence – led us immediately into our paradise, enclosed by the palings. Five or six oak steps up, a narrow sill, then three steps down the other side – there was only that delightful clamber between us and bliss. Substantial hand-rails to the stile had received letterings from many pocket knives and grown dark brown with years of weather and of hand-clutchings, and the treads too were dark and worn. For hither converged many public foot-ways across the Park – from Hoghatch, from Hungry Hill, from Hale – for Farnham town; and it was not only children like ourselves who used that stile; but town loiterers and tradesfolk out for a walk, and labourers going to and from their work. Besides our soft "puddies", the hardened palms of grown-up people – sawyers, hop-ground diggers, carpenters, brick-makers and bricklayers, to specify but a few – had helped to make those hand-rails all dark and shiny.'

❧ HAMBLEDON

A law of the land had its origins in Hambledon back in 1933 when the members of the Women's Institute branch won the approval of their colleagues from all over the country on the question of the sale of live English wild birds. Hambledon's resolution was passed unanimously by 8,000 women attending the Institute's national conference in the Albert Hall, and later that year a bill was adopted by the Government, under the Prime Minister, Mr Ramsay Macdonald, and became law. But the original credit went to the women of Hambledon for bringing the matter to the notice of the public at large. The motion was proposed by the daughter of the author Eric Parker, who lived at Feathercombe in the village, but sadly his wife, who was president of the WI branch, died on that very day, having collapsed the previous day while travelling to London by train to hear her daughter speak in the Albert Hall.

A clay track through Hambledon Hurst was the old highway between Godalming and Chiddingfold and was continually presented as being out of repair in Godalming Hundred courts in the 14th, 15th and 16th centuries. On 21 September 1340, Thomas le Beel, rector of Hambledon, came before the court for digging a ditch in the highway.

Nowadays, Hambledon is remembered for its brick-making; centuries ago iron was mined, hence the name Mine Pits Copse. The ore was claimed by Lord Montague who ran into a spot of bother in February 1570 when commoners resented his cutting the woods for his works.

In the 1930s there was great concern when the Godalming Fire Brigade refused to attend a rick blaze in the village. The reason? The owner of the rick was not a subscriber to the brigade. There was alarm in the village when it was discovered the parish council had also not been supporting the brigade, which would be within its rights not to attend a house fire. The outcome? It was suggested that Hambledon enter into an agreement with Guildford 'as the contribution was lower than that required by Godalming, and the extra four miles made very little difference with a motor fire engine', reported the *Haslemere Herald*.

St Peter's church sits on a knoll and within its ground are two venerable yews, one of them hollow and the subject of a piece of Surrey folklore. It was said that if you walked three times around the inside of the hollow tree you would see a witch.

Hambledon is an out-of-the-way place which, until the mid-1970s, lent its name to the local authority. Hambledon Rural District Council was one of the bodies which was swallowed up when the Local Government Commission reorganised the boundaries. Waverley District Council was the new baby, and in 1984 a royal charter gave it borough status and thus a mayor.

The name of Hambledon RDC lives on in plaques attached to buildings and bridges and, for the very observant, official notices.

🍁 HASCOMBE

How many of the thousands of visitors who annually walk through the glades and groves of Winkworth Arboretum between Busbridge and Hascombe know how such a beautiful and tranquil spot came to be there? The National Trust owns it but the majority of its 100 acres was the creation of one man who, when he bought the then steep hillside covered in hazel scrub and coppice, knew nothing about gardening.

It was in 1938 that Dr Wilfrid Fox, senior consultant at St George's Hospital in London and the outstanding dermatologist of his age, bought Winkworth Farm. He had no interest in gardening but was prepared to learn; he was a man who achieved many things in his life. Soon he founded the Roads Beautifying Association, born out of his despair at daily seeing the barren roadside along the new Kingston bypass.

When the doctor went to Austria on holiday in 1938 land adjoining his home became available for purchase. Telegrams went back and forth and the scrubby hillside was bought. The messages, it was said, attracted the interest of the Germans who thought they were in code. Dr Fox returned from the Continent and with unbridled energy set about transforming the landscape. He did the digging himself, with the help of a retired woodman and occasional parties of friends. Tree planting began with a maple grove for autumn colouring and an azalea glade based on a garden beside Dr Fox's beloved Lake Como.

In 1952 the 60 acres were given to the National Trust which five years later bought an adjoining 35 acres. At the foot of the wooded hillside is a lake and beyond, in a valley, is the hamlet of Thorncombe Street with some pleasant and mellow cottages. Dr Fox died in 1962, two days after returning from Lake Como. 'I want to see it once more before I die,' he had said. Appropriately, the funeral service was in the church of St John the Baptist at Busbridge, in whose churchyard 30 years earlier was buried that great gardener Gertrude Jekyll. Dr Fox's old home, Winkworth Farm, is now in the hands of the artist David Shepherd, known for his elephant paintings, love of steam trains and conservation work.

Hascombe seems to be cut off from the outside world. It is a beautiful village surrounded by heavily wooded hillsides. The trees have been noted by a succession of writers. One in the 19th century said of the chestnuts at Burgate: 'Such a bit of Spain as it would be difficult to parallel this side of the Pyrenees.' Those chestnuts are now on private property, but

A leafy Surrey lane.

there are others, especially along the winding lanes of the village towards Hydon Ball, a curiously named beauty spot which, from its 593ft summit, offers superb views over the Weald.

Eric Parker thought the yews in the churchyard would one day be famous but, alas, he was wrong. They are no longer there, apart from a small archway at the gate. St Peter's church was rebuilt in the mid-1800s and is tucked away behind the village street in a peaceful setting. Opposite is the village pond and an old cottage which was once an almshouse. Nearby, the White Horse formerly had a sign painted by Gertrude Jekyll, who trained as an artist although she was more renowned in these parts for her gardens which complemented many Lutyens designed houses.

Hascombe Hill is 51ft higher than Hydon Ball and was important as a telegraph station at the dawn of the 19th century (much earlier it was an Iron Age fortress). For 20 years the shutter system of sending messages between the Admiralty and Portsmouth involved a great deal of manpower, and the Hascombe telegraphists were a vital link in the chain.

On 30 June 1579 at Kingston Assizes Thomas Hedger was sentenced to hang for sheep stealing. He was a Hascombe butcher and was found guilty, with a Cranleigh man, William Kerrey, of stealing 69 sheep. Kerrey was handed over to the clergy. Later he was indicted on similar offences but, according to the record, was 'at large' at the time of his scheduled appearance in the dock.

🍁 HAXTED

A hamlet in the parish of Lingfield within a mile of the Kent border, and visited by large numbers of people because of its watermill museum. Haxted mill dates from 1580 but, according to the will of Reginald de Cobham of Starborough Castle, there was a mill in the 14th century. Jack Hillier, in his *Old Surrey Watermills*, published in 1951, said of Haxted: 'The miller was shocked and scathing when I suggested the age of his mill to be two or three hundred years. "Two or three hundred? It's nine hundred years old. It's mentioned in Domesday".' Mr Hillier said he was usually inclined to smile at the notion 'commonly held by millers who have heard of their mill's inclusion in the Domesday survey and presume the buildings are the selfsame that William's assessors recorded'. He considered that at Haxted no remnant of a Saxon mill could exist but because 'the timbers are of that great bulk and rough, sturdy adze shaping, that some may go back to a very early date indeed – fifteenth or sixteenth century, perhaps'. Jack Hillier, who was the foremost expert on Japanese prints outside Japan, was the son of a Fulham postman, and died in January 1995, aged 82. His book is a valuable piece of research into a way of life in the county long since gone, and copies rarely appear on the open market.

The mill at Haxted was always a corn mill and ground flour until 1919, and then meal for farmers until its working life ended in 1945. Haxted opened as a museum in 1969, since which time the waterwheel and mill race have been restored. The wheel, which is about 150 years old, is powered by the Eden, which is generally regarded as a Kent river but, in fact, rises in Surrey in the countryside around Oxted to the south of the North Downs.

❧ HEADLEY

The M25 motorway cuts through the countryside between Headley and its neighbour Walton-on-the-Hill. The section of

London's orbital bypass between Reigate and Wisley took a long time to be completed and was opened in 1985.

Headley, high up on the chalk, attracted Aubrey on one of his perambulations, and he wrote: 'The shepherds of these Downs use a half-horn, slit length way, nailed to the end of a long staff with which they can hurl a stone to a great distance and so keep their sheep within their bounds, or from straggling into the corn.' And William Bray, who completed the massive county history begun by the Rev Owen Manning, spoke to a man in 1808 who remembered, 40 years earlier, shepherds in the area who could hit sheep at a distance of 20 rods (357 ft).

The church of St Mary the Virgin is Victorian but evidence of an earlier building can be seen over the grave of one of the 19th century incumbents, the Rev Ferdinand Faithfull, who died in 1871. Faithfull's daughter, Emily, who was born in 1835, became printer and publisher to Queen Victoria after she had gone to London and set up a printing press.

🍁 HEATH END

The former Halfway House pub on the main road at Heath End probably owes its name to the First World War, perhaps much earlier. It has been suggested that it was halfway between the railway station at Farnham and the military centre at North Camp, Farnborough, and troops on the march to or from the trains welcomed its appearance through the dust and dirt of a weary trek. A photograph that has appeared from time to time in the *Farnham Herald* has shown the Halfway House in 1905 as a building whose doors opened directly on to a dusty road. Opposite was a bakery and a tea room. Now the road is choked by fast-moving vehicles, in spite of the fact that the Blackwater Valley Road is supposed to take through traffic away from residential areas, and local residents are rightly concerned about the associated dangers. Their campaign for an improvement is linked to the need to find a better road system around Farnham, a requirement heightened by the extra traffic generated by the BVR. As for the Halfway House, its name was changed to the Blues Tavern but its fortunes were not, and its doors were closed in 1998.

🍁 HERSHAM

A suburb of Walton-on-Thames whose common was enclosed in 1804 by an Act of Parliament, which gave the signal for developers to take an interest. Wealthy Londoners had villas built at Hersham in the 1820s, the railway arrived in 1838 and soon a busy and thriving community was established. A nonconformist chapel went up in 1844 but St Peter's church was not built for another 43 years. The chapel has been demolished as has its neighbour, Rookwood, a circular cottage built with the trunks of gnarled trees.

🍁 HINCHLEY WOOD

Suburban Surrey beside the Kingston bypass. In fact, the area was settled when the new road opened it up in the late 1920s, and when the railway station was opened the name Hinchley Wood (already in use for a local group of trees) became accepted. Telegraph Hill was known as Cooper's Hill in the days when there was a semaphore station there in the early 1800s.

🍁 HINDHEAD

People know Hindhead today as a place to avoid. The traffic problems associated with the crossroads where the A287 intersects the A3 get worse and there is no end in sight. Since before the Second World War, Hindhead has been a motorists' nightmare, and a corridor of land was retained for road improvements. Successive governments have failed to grasp the nettle, with the result that the settlement around the cross-roads has all but had the life squeezed out of it. The current scheme is for a tunnel to be bored under Gibbet Hill and Hindhead Common, but the cost of this is sufficient to make any transport minister prevaricate long enough for it to become someone else's decision. The anti-tunnel lobby wants an overland alternative, but the experience of an ill-fated Red Route in the mid-1980s, when a score of properties was compulsorily purchased and the National Trust dug its heels in at the suggestion of a viaduct across the Devil's Punch Bowl, leads people to believe that any solution is still a long way off.

The founder of modern Hindhead was Professor John Tyndall, an eminent scientist of the 19th century who, in the

1880s, came to the conclusion, in the way that scientists do, that the air at Hindhead was every bit as good as that at Bel Alp in Switzerland, which he had been in the habit of visiting for long periods. So he built a house 'four square to the winds of heaven' and close to the crossroads which were already well known to travellers on the London to Portsmouth road because of the presence of the Royal Huts Hotel.

Tyndall's enthusiasm for Hindhead soon encouraged other notable people to make the place their home. George Bernard Shaw came to Blen Cathra (now a school), a little way south on the Portsmouth road, and Sir Arthur Conan Doyle built a house (now a hotel) opposite the Royal Huts and called it Undershaw. A.J. Balfour, who was to become Prime Minister, owned land next to Tyndall's. These great men, and several others, needed staff and gradually Hindhead began to take on the appearance of a village. Shops sprang up around the cross-roads and villas were built at Beacon Hill, a mile north of the A3.

Large hotels were built and Hindhead, which had once been a notoriously inhospitable spot and given a bad press by William Cobbett, was the 'in' place. Tyndall's home is now flats and surrounded by a housing estate which bears his name. The Royal Huts Hotel is, alas, no more, but locals still refer to the place as 'The Huts' in spite of the building's change of name and role as a branch of a roadside restaurant chain.

While modern Hindhead is barely older than the 20th century, there was a settlement in the mid-1800s. The census of 1861 reveals 44 people living there, and with the exception of the innkeeper and, perhaps not surprisingly in view of Cobbett's observations on the place 40 years earlier that it was 'the most villainous spot God ever made', a policeman, all the men were either broom-makers or agricultural labourers. One family of 12 living in the Devil's Punch Bowl earned their money from three sources. Father and eldest son, aged 15, were broom-makers;

mother and the two older daughters, aged 19 and 17, were woolspinners; while a 13-year-old son was a shoemaker.

The Devil's Punch Bowl, which is in Thursley parish, and Gibbet Hill, forever linked to a grisly murder more than 200 years ago, whose story began and ended in Thursley, have been in the care of the National Trust for many years. Indeed, much of Hindhead is controlled by the Trust and long may that continue. There is undoubtedly more pollution in the air than in Tyndall's day, but it is still possible to breathe in the freshness of the pines which grow so well on the greensand. The Punch Bowl was the home of many families whose names can still be found in the area. In the more recent past they were broom-makers; earlier they were charcoal burners working in conjunction with the iron masters of the district.

HOLMBURY ST MARY

'This is heaven's gate!' exclaimed the wife of the celebrated Victorian architect George Edward Street, as the couple's carriage brought them to this upland village in 1872. They were on a visit to friends at The Aldermoor on the side of Holmbury Hill, and there and then, it seems, they decided they wanted a house there, too. So they built Holmdale. The village was called Felday in those days and only changed to its present name after Mr Street had designed and paid for a parish church.

G.E. Street, whose London designs include the Law Courts, was clearly a man of considerable standing, and when he died he was buried in Westminster Abbey. In 1880 his home in the village was visited by Gladstone, the Prime Minister, and members of the Cabinet.

St Mary's, which was built in 1879, looks down on the village which nestles around a green. It is not hard to imagine it as it was a century and more ago. The area was one of the wildest in the county, and sheep stealers, smugglers and poachers took refuge in the remote hills. Many of the cottages had large cellars where the contraband was hidden.

Holmbury Hill, which Aubrey called a mountain, is, in fact, 857ft above sea level which leaves it short of Hindhead and Leith Hill. There was an early British camp there and Guildford Museum has a collection of artefacts found when the site was excavated in the 1930s.

Like all of the Surrey hills, it is magnificent walking country, and the views across the Weald to the South Downs are breathtaking.

🍁 HOLMWOOD

Wild Holmwood Common was the haunt of highwaymen and smugglers. Now it is owned by the National Trust, thanks to a gift by the Duke of Norfolk in 1956, and is altogether a much more hospitable place. The common separates North and South Holmwood; the former is nearer Dorking and suffers as a result of the urban sprawl moving its way.

When James II was the Duke of York the largest stags in England were hunted at Holmwood. Wild boar, too, were pursued to the death, and wild strawberries were plentiful and taken to market by the horse load.

A turnpike road from London to Horsham ran across the common and highway robbers were everywhere. The *Victoria County History* records a man who died in 1902 aged 101 having a workmate who had witnessed a turnpike keeper boldly refusing to open his gate at night to a group of smugglers with kegs of brandy on their horses.

South Holmwood's St Mary Magdalene church was built in 1838 and the site for it, a parsonage and a school was given by the Duke of Norfolk.

The *Surrey Advertiser* reported that a great storm that blew 80 mph winds across the country on the weekend of 18-19 February 1910 led to the death of a Holmwood man. Charles Green, of Holly Green, was drowned with another man, from London, when a rowing boat capsized at Burnham-on-Crouch in Essex. He was the owner of a yacht called *Alice* and with two other men had been obtaining provisions in the village, and was rowing back to the yacht which was moored about a quarter of a mile from the shore. A sudden gust of wind overturned the boat and all three men were thrown into the water. Mr Green and one of the others were strong swimmers, but their companion could not swim and, in an attempt to save him, he and Mr Green lost their lives. The third man was saved.

🍁 HORNE

Hardly a village at all, more a collection of buildings including a church and a school. St Mary's was a chapel of ease to Bletchingley until 1706 but in 1880 it underwent 'pitiful renewal and restoration', say Pevsner and Nairn.

🍁 HORSELL

There is still something of a village atmosphere about Horsell, in spite of the ever-growing tentacles of Woking, a town which grew with the railway and has consumed so much as residents and businesses have demanded more land for bricks and mortar. But Horsell is just beyond the fringe – at the moment. When the railway first came to the neighbourhood Horsell was so secluded that a place near the canal was selected as a suitable venue for a prize fight. The rich gentlemen came out from London on the train and were conveyed to the ringside which

THE SURREY VILLAGE BOOK ■ HORSELL

was out of the observation range of the police in Woking.

The church of St Mary is 14th century and stands in a pleasant churchyard. Until the beginning of the 20th century Horsell comprised a single street surrounded by nurseries. The Cricketers Inn has been used at times as a lock-up, poor house, hospital, school and store. In the mid-19th century a windmill drove a saw pit.

Britain's Muslim community has long been associated with Woking and there was a cemetery on Horsell Common. It was created in 1915 for Indian soldiers who died during the First World War, but after vandalism in the 1950s the bodies were exhumed and buried elsewhere. The Muslim connection with Woking is more than 100 years old, for it was in 1884 that a Dr Gottlieb Wilhelm Leitner, at one time principal of Punjab University, secured a building in Maybury, a district of Woking, that had been used as a college of drama. A mosque was erected nearer the turn of the century and is still used although the Leitner building has been swallowed by industry.

There were Martians on Horsell Common in 1898, or so H.G. Wells would have us believe in *The War of the Worlds*. Wells lived in Woking for a time and he had the Martians and their machine landing near a sandpit on the common. Wells died in 1946 which was the year the Horsell Common Preservation Society, formed in 1910, obtained a 99-year lease on the 750 acres. The society later secured the freehold.

A piece of modern sculpture was placed in the centre of Woking in 1998 to mark the centenary of *The War of the Worlds*.

🍁 HORSLEY, EAST

Like the Clandons to the west, the Horsleys are twin villages with many pleasant, rural features. East Horsley, when approached from Guildford, comes upon the traveller in the form of the gatehouse to Horsley Towers, a quite unusual building for this part of the country. The present Towers dates from the mid-1800s when most of East Horsley was rebuilt under the direction of the Earl of Lovelace. The entrance to Horsley Towers, which has been a training and management centre for some years, stands on a sharp bend in the road, which then twists again and heads off for Effingham. East Horsley's church is dedicated to St Martin and there cannot be too many of those around.

There are two distinct parts to the village, that close to the Towers, with its parade of shops, and a far busier centre near the station. The village suffers from constant traffic, but away from the through road are quiet areas. The superbly appointed village hall is a credit to the fund-raising efforts of the community, and beside it is a large recreational space.

🍁 HORSLEY, WEST

West Horsley was, it seems, first mentioned in the ninth century and the church of St Mary the Virgin has some pre-Conquest work. Sir Walter Raleigh's head is supposed to be buried in a vault under the south chapel, having been preserved in a red leather bag for 25 years by his widow and then interred along with his son, Carew, who had inherited West Horsley Place in 1643. The claim appeared to be substantiated by William Nicholas who, when burying his mother, Penelope, stated there was a head revealed in the vault which was apart from any body or other remains.

Penelope Nicholas lost her life when a chimney was brought crashing down on to her bed during the Great Storm of Saturday, 26 November 1703 – the storm which wrecked 15 warships, demolished the Eddystone lighthouse, killed the Bishop of Bath and Wells in his palace, and devastated London to the tune of one million pounds.

West Horsley Place has a fascinating if macabre history. One of its earlier occupants was Sir James Berners, a follower of Richard II, who was beheaded on Tower Hill in 1388. His daughter was Dame Juliana Berners who part-wrote the *Boke of St Albans* – a 'Treatyse perteynynge to Hawkynge, Huntynge, Fysshynge and Coote Armiris'. A later owner was the Marquis of Exeter who also lost his life on Tower Hill for plotting to murder the King in 1538. And the Earl of Surrey, whose poems about 'Fair Geraldine' were of 13-year-old Elizabeth Fitzgerald, later widow of Sir Anthony Browne of West Horsley Place, lost his head five years after he penned his amorous lines.

🍁 HURTMORE

Hurtmore is an area long associated with the soil. Market gardening dominated the landscape for decades, and it was the home of Roy Hay, a leading gardening writer and broadcaster in the days before television made growing things such a big business. The place was mentioned in the Domesday Book as Hormera and its mill was valued at 11s. Modern Hurtmore is bypassed by the A3, from which a slip road takes traffic en route to Charterhouse School at Godalming.

🍁 HYDESTILE

There were at one time three hospitals at Hydestile which is a loosely defined area about Hambledon and beyond the outlying station at Milford. King George V Hospital was opened in 1922 by the Metropolitan Asylums Board as a sanatorium for TB patients from London. It had as many as 232 beds in its heyday, but in 1969 its chest work was transferred to Milford Chest Hospital and a unit for mentally handicapped adults was established. The Chest Hospital had been opened in 1928 by the then Minister of Health, Neville Chamberlain. The site had been purchased in 1914 but the war interrupted plans and it was not until 11 years later that building commenced. It was originally known as the Surrey County Sanatorium and administered by the county council until 1948. There were 300 beds in six blocks at its peak period. The third hospital to open was Hydestile in 1940, as a hutted annexe to its neighbour, King George V. There are plaques which recall the occupancy of the hospital by members of the 3rd Australian General Hospital in 1940-41 and as a 'tribute to the very gallant part the Commonwealth forces took in the Second World War'. A second plaque bears the arms of St Thomas's Hospital and records: 'St Thomas's Hospital moved here in April 1941 during the bombing of London, leaving behind a casualty and emergency service. After the war, owing to the loss of accommodation through air raids, Hydestile was retained as a branch hospital until March 1968. The governors and staff record their appreciation of the warmth of the local hospitality.' Hydestile subsequently cared for geriatric patients and the young chronic sick, and was also a day hospital. When the medical services pulled out, the site became increasingly derelict and, after hotly contested planning applications, some housing has been allowed.

Milford Hospital is on a back road to Godalming which passes through Tuesley where there are some picturesque buildings. In earlier times Minster Field in Tuesley was the site of a church, and a chapel dedicated to the Virgin Mary was in ruins there in 1220.

Beyond Hydestile is Hydon Ball, the 593ft hill which was donated to the National Trust as a memorial to Octavia Hill, a co-founder of the Trust and a social reformer, who died in 1912. Three years later a party of her friends climbed to the top and watched the unveiling of a granite seat, upon which a plate recorded that it was given in memory of Octavia Hill who was born in 1838.

Hydon Ball is one of a trio of hills in the area, Hascombe and Hambledon are the others, and there is an odd rhyme attached to it:

On Hydon's top there is a cup
And in that cup there is a drop
Pick up the cup, and drink the drop
And place the cup on Hydon's top.

Guildford Museum has a record of a Scottish verse in similar vein:

On Tinto's top there is a mist
And in the mist there is a kist
And in the kist there is a cup
Take up the cup and drink the drop
And then come down from Tinto's top.

🍁 Jacobs Well

There has been a good deal of speculation about the origins of the name Jacobs Well, which is in the parish of Worplesdon. According to the curator of Guildford Museum it first appeared on the Worplesdon tithe map of 1839. But although there are wells in the area there is, as yet, no evidence of a local inhabitant called Jacob who might have lent his name to the place.

Separated from Guildford by the A3, and in spite of being close to the industrial estate at Slyfield, Jacobs Well has got its own identity. However, traffic is a problem, particularly on the Woking road where tree protesters camped for several weeks in 1997 to hold up work on a realignment scheme. In the end, the county council decided that the project could not be funded, but the tree people claimed a victory all the same.

🍁 Kingswood

This was once a well-wooded hamlet but it is now built up and handy enough to the capital to make it popular with commuters. The church of St Andrew was built in 1852 and replaced one put up in 1835 soon after the village became a separate parish. In Lower Kingswood, the church of St Sophia was built in 1891 by two men who rejoiced in the names of Dr Edwin Freshfield and Sir Cosmo Bonsor and is, say Pevsner and Nairn, a 'most remarkable church, more even for its contents than its architecture'. Dr Freshfield brought the upper part of nine Byzantine columns to Lower Kingswood, three from St John at Ephesus, which are either fourth or sixth century, and the others from Constantinople.

🍁 KNAPHILL

To the north of Knaphill, which is on the western outskirts of Woking, is Hill Place, a manor house that was first mentioned in the 14th century. In 600 years, its owners have been numerous, including King Henry VIII and Sir William More, the builder of Loseley House near Guildford. But for almost 250 years the property was owned by the Collyers, who were prominent yeoman farmers. Henry Collyer of Old Woking bought Hill Place for £600 on 18 December 1621, and his great-great-great grandson William sold it to a Godalming man in 1841. Some of the later Collyers were nurserymen, and this fits well with Knaphill, which has long been known for its nurseries, including those of the Waterer family, famous for rhododendrons.

🍁 LALEHAM

Dr Arnold loved this Thames-side village which came into Surrey from Middlesex in the 1970s. He lived and taught privately here from 1819 to 1828 before moving to the headship of Rugby School and immortality. Thomas Arnold often thought fondly of Laleham as a passage in his biography confirmed: 'Years after he left Laleham he still retained his early affection for it, and till he had purchased his house in Westmorland he entertained a lingering hope that he might return to it in his old age, when he retired from Rugby.' Matthew Arnold, the teacher's son who was a poet among other literary attributes, was born in Laleham in 1822 and was buried in the churchyard of All Saints, alongside his three brothers who died in childhood. Matthew returned often and once wrote to his mother: 'I was at the old house and under the cedars and by the big pink acacia.' The house was demolished in 1864 and some of the bricks were used to build a school.

Laleham Abbey and its 70 acres are in use as a public recreation ground and camping site. It was built in 1803 as Laleham House for the Earl of Lucan who led the Heavy Brigade at Balaclava.

🍁 LEIGH

This small village near Reigate is where the poet, dramatist and friend of Shakespeare, Ben Jonson, is said to have spent much of his retirement. Leigh, pronounced 'Lye', has an attractive green at its centre with the weatherboarded Plough Inn on one side. Many of the houses are said to be constructed of timbers originally grown in the great oak forests of the district and sawn in earlier times for the manufacture of sailing ships. St Bartholomew's church is small and without aisles, and until 1890 had a timber belfry. That was followed by a stone tower and later a bellcote was added.

🍁 LIGHTWATER

An area known to drivers as a place to avoid during rush-hours because of the M3 intersection with the A322 – a busy road between Guildford and the Thames Valley that offers an alternative to the congestion of the M25 and its junction with the M4 near Heathrow. But away from the traffic, Lightwater Country Park is an excellent open space with a visitor centre and many interesting trails to follow.

A well known landmark in Limpsfield.

🍁 LIMPSFIELD

Surrey disappears here where the A25 runs on into Kent. Limpsfield, its common and neighbouring Limpsfield Chart nestle below the Downs. The main street through Limpsfield runs at right angles to the A25 and is full of half-timbered houses and little nooks and crannies. On the common, that great pioneer aviator Col Samuel Cody first flew his man-lifting kites, while Lord Baden Powell had an experimental airstrip there.

One writer observed of Limpsfield: 'The village street always strikes me as the place swept by eyes of elderly ladies determined to pounce upon any stray piece of paper, eyes that would blaze reproach at the sight of a lump of builders' sand obstructing the pathway.'

The composer Frederick Delius is buried in the churchyard of St Peter's. Born in Yorkshire in 1862, he lived most of his life in France where he died in 1934. He was buried in France but the following year his body was brought back to England and re-buried at Limpsfield, where Sir Thomas Beecham, who had been a major influence in bringing the work of Delius to a wider audience, led a torchlight funeral oration. The composer's wife is also buried in the churchyard, as is Harriet Kennard who, at the age of 80, nursed men constructing the railway when there was an outbreak of cholera. She, too, died from the disease.

Limpsfield was mentioned in the Domesday Book as being held by the Abbot of Battle. William the Conqueror's surveyors found, among other things, a mill, fishery and church, two stone quarries, and three hawks' nests in the woodland.

Aubrey noted the 'delicate, wholesome and sweet air' of the district, and perhaps this accounted for 12-year-old John Brasie becoming the hero of a cricket match when he made a

Limpsfield.

match-winning score of 84 against local rivals Oxted. The celebrations that followed included a march down the village street
led by a brass band lent by the rector.

🍁 LINGFIELD

Racing at Lingfield brings this village in the south-east of the county into public focus, particularly now that an all-weather track allows the sport to continue throughout the year. The racecourse was established in 1890 and is to the south of the village in gentle country not far from the borders of Kent and Sussex.

The delight of Lingfield is the church of St Peter and St Paul and its southern approach through a narrow lane of buildings. The church has many memorials to the great Cobham family who lived at nearby Starborough Castle. They fought for King and Country, and Richard, the second Lord Cobham, in his will in 1417, founded a college close to the church for a provost, six chaplains, four clerks, and 13 poor persons. It remained until 1544 when King Henry VIII had other ideas. The village library is now based in what was the college's guest house.

In the centre of the village is The Cage, once the lock-up. It was last used 100 years or so ago, and in 1850 figured in a dramatic escape when 11 poachers were being held overnight. While the police constable on guard duty dozed off, the poachers' friends stole up under the cover of darkness and removed the roof to free the captives. The Cage is beside a hollow oak and next to the village pond, but the overall setting is of the urban nineties: houses, shops and traffic.

A fascinating little booklet by the late Gordon Jenner, entitled *The Lingfield I Knew*, tells of how one group of villagers was prepared for the start of the First World War. A Lieut Lockyer, said Mr Jenner, was playing cricket on 3 August 1914, when the local telegraph boy arrived with a message which he handed to Lockyer. The officer walked over to his skipper and departed for the pavilion. The other players were told that Lockyer had been recalled to his regiment, and stumps were drawn. The next day war was declared.

🍁 LITTLETON (Guildford)

A hamlet off the beaten track but only a mile or so from Guildford High Street. Here is Loseley, one of the grandest Elizabethan houses in England. Built at a cost of £1,640 with material from the dissolved abbey at Waverley by Sir William More in the 1560s, it continues to be owned by the same family who, through marriage, are now More-Molyneux. The estate had been purchased in 1508 by Sir William's father, Sir Christopher. There was a west wing which was believed to have been added around 1600, but it became derelict and was demolished before the halfway point of the 19th century. Loseley, thank goodness, has never become a stately home and therefore the visits that are permitted during the summer months are a joy to make. A tithe barn, thought to have been constructed in about 1633 and rescued from Conduit Farm on the estate and reassembled on its present site in 1982, is a popular venue for functions, and allows many more people the opportunity to enjoy the external features of the great house. Standing close to the North Downs Way, it was in fact a hay barn and a straw barn, both of six bays. Surrey Domestic Buildings Research Group discovered in 1977 that many of the timbers in the hay barn had previously been used, probably in ships.

Littleton is the estate village with attractive cottages and the church of St Francis which was once a dame school, founded in 1843 by the More-Molyneux family. It was used as such until 1904 when the children moved to a new school and the building was converted into a church. Littleton Lane, narrow between banks of wild flowers and tall hedges and used by motorists as a 'rat run' in an attempt to avoid the busy road between Guildford and Godalming, heads for the county town but not before it passes a track which affords an access onto the Pilgrims' Way and the North Downs Way.

🍁 LITTLETON (Spelthorne)

There are 7,000 million gallons of water on Littleton's doorstep. When Queen Mary Reservoir was opened in 1925 acres of fields, woods and cottages were submerged. It was then the largest reservoir of its kind in the world and a breakwater was constructed to restrain the water in high winds. Littleton, which came into Surrey in 1974, was first mentioned in 1042 but did not appear in the Domesday Book because it was attached to Laleham. The manor broke away from Laleham in the 12th century and had a number of owners who lived at Littleton Park until the mansion was burned down in 1974. Since rebuilt, it is now a film studio. The building is close to St Mary Magdalene church which has a 13th century chancel and a tower that was built between the 16th and 18th centuries. There is a stained glass window of a painting by Sir John Millais which was given by his widow. Sir John often stayed at the Rectory which was built in 1699.

❧ LYNE

The almoner of Chertsey Abbey lived at Almners Priory in this hamlet to the west of Chertsey where Holy Trinity church is picturesque and early Victorian. The Benedictine abbey of St Peter, Chertsey, was founded in AD 666 by Erkenwald who subsequently became Bishop of London. The site was marshy and desolate and in the 10th century had to be refounded after the Danes had invaded it. By the time of the Domesday survey the abbey owned lands elsewhere in Surrey plus Hampshire and Berkshire. Expansion took place in the 12th century, oak trees were planted, fishponds constructed, and a bridge was built, which is still in use in Guildford Street, Chertsey. The Dissolution came in 1537 and Henry VIII's mason, John Nedeham, took some of the material for Hampton Court the following year. Excavations have taken place but to all intents and purposes the abbey has been lost for good.

St Ann's Hill, which rises to 240ft, is a popular spot with walkers who can see St Paul's Cathedral on a clear day. It was presented to the public in 1928 by Sir William Berry. On the southern slopes was an estate owned by the politician Charles James Fox, and this, too, is open to the public.

🍁 MAYFORD

This is no more than a suburb of Woking, but it is separated from Surrey's largest town by a wedge of green land. And when Mayford is approached from Guildford, the roundabout close to the Bird in Hand public house clearly announces that it will not be long before the driver is plunged into Woking's heavily built-up heart.

In 1972 Mayford History Society published a booklet whose contents were later to haunt its members. *And so to Mainford: A Woking Diary of 1830* purported to be the work of Charlotte Bowles, sister of Charles Bowles, one-time vicar of Woking, but it turned out to be a hoax. When it appeared its authenticity was not questioned, and it was not until November 1976, when historian and artist John Baker, in one of his regular columns published in the *Surrey Advertiser*, drew attention to various inaccuracies and inconsistencies, that a local teacher turned detective. What he discovered led a 20-year-old man to confess that five years earlier he had faked the diary which had fooled experts into believing that he had found a long-lost piece of history.

The introduction to the booklet records that in the summer of 1971, the young man, a member of Mayford History Society and 'a collector of Victoriana', was looking through a mid-19th century cookery book in an antique shop in Woking. 'Between its pages he found, inserted at random and tightly folded, 12 sheets of unglazed white quarto notepaper, closely written on both sides, which appeared to be extracts from an anonymous diary.' When the truth was out, the hoaxer admitted that the elaborate deception had got completely out of hand. He had found 'about three' loose sheets of writing in the book. The booklet, indistinguishable from many other local history publications, rapidly became a collector's item. It is seldom seen today in second-hand bookshops.

🍁 MERROW

'There runs a road by Merrow Down – A grassy track today it is – An hour out of Guildford town, Above the river Wey it is.' Merrow Downs were famous long before Kipling wrote those lines. Great horse races took place there, and early cricket matches, too. Now, the Downs are a favourite haunt of ramblers, who have to keep a look out for players on Guildford golf course...

Merrow village has taken on the role of Guildford suburb, but the old church of St John the Evangelist which dates from the middle of the 12th century but fell badly into restorers' hands more than 150 years ago, and the Horse and Groom public house, with a 1615 date on the exterior, stand resolutely amid the new buildings.

There was a public well opposite the inn which was more than 100ft deep. Buried in the churchyard is one Walter Broke, gent, who died aged 107 in 1603. It is said that when past his 100th birthday he walked from Merrow to London in a day.

But Merrow will always be known for its Downs. The best way to approach them is by foot but for the motorists the old road, up Trodds Lane from the church, is the prettiest. At the summit is Newlands Corner where John St Loe Strachey, proprietor and editor of the *Spectator* for the first quarter of the 20th century, built a house which later became a hotel.

The views are magnificent, as they must have been to the race-goers who flocked to the Downs during Whit week. William III had given a King's Plate of 100 guineas which lapsed under Queen Anne but was renewed by George I. In Victoria's reign it was given as a Queen's Plate. The meeting used to fill Guildford with visitors, but the growth of Epsom and the establishment of Ascot gradually caused a winding down of proceedings. The grandstand was demolished around 1850.

Mr W.C. Smith, in his *Rambles Round Guildford*, 1828, wrote of the Downs: 'This place was famous some 20 or 30 years ago for the races held here, and so great was the concourse of people who then visited Guildford, that very exorbitant sums were not infrequently paid for lodgings and other accommodations during the week.'

Much earlier on Merrow Downs, in 1601, there was a fearful accident during a course of training which left three men dead following a munitions explosion.

🍁 MERSTHAM

Surrey's own Spaghetti Junction, where the M25 and M23 meet, is near Merstham. The high-level interchange and its numerous junctions are cut into the chalk of the North Downs and are a far cry from the village's quaintly named Quality Street. The North Downs Way passes through Merstham whose sandstone quarries provided material for the building of Windsor Castle in the middle of the 14th century, as well as London Bridge, St Paul's Cathedral and for work at Westminster. The church of St Katherine is 13th century, while the lych gate is believed to have been made with timbers from an old mill that was demolished to make way for the railway. The first public railway in the country was in Merstham; horse-drawn wagons carrying stone and lime from the quarries to the river Thames at Wandsworth in the early part of the 19th century.

🍁 MICKLEHAM

This is Fanny Burney country. The daughter of Dr Charles Burney, scholar and musician, was born in Norfolk in 1752 but established herself as a novelist in Surrey. Fanny wrote *Evelina* while staying at Chessington, and it was this work that made her a force in the literary world. In 1786 she became Second Keeper of the Robes to Queen Charlotte, a position which, it seems, put her under great strain and after five years she was granted retirement. It proved to be the turning point in her life that she was looking for, and in the following year she met her future husband, the French general Alexandre Gabriel Jean-Baptiste D'Arblay, whom she married in St Michael's church at Mickleham. Fanny's first meeting with the general was at Juniper Hall, Mickleham, which had become a centre for emigrés from the French Revolution (and is now a field studies centre). After her marriage, Fanny wrote, among other things, *Camilla* which earned her enough money to build a home at Westhumble. They called it Camilla Cottage and today it is remembered by Camilla Lacey, a housing estate in that village.

🍁 MILFORD

The commons to the south of Milford were home to thousands of Canadian soldiers during the wars. Now they are nature reserves and conservation areas beloved of walkers and riders. The late Ted Chambers, who died early in 1984, was responsible for turning overgrown wasteland into something that can now be enjoyed by everyone.

Milford has a station on the London to Portsmouth line half a mile from the village centre. A bypass completed in the 1980s has relieved the heavy congestion at the village traffic lights. It is part of the parish of Witley but became a separate ecclesiastical parish more than 150 years ago when St John's church was built.

The churchyard contains a mausoleum for the Webbs who lived at Milford House, a big, square building dating back to 1730 which became a hotel, was severely damaged by fire some years ago and had remained an eyesore until recently, when work began on converting the ruin into apartments. On the Godalming side of Milford House is the Refectory which was a barn, with a claim to being 11th century, before being converted à la Lutyens in the 1930s. Authentic Lutyens can be observed in Rake Manor near the station which was an early 17th century building.

The old A3 swings past Mousehill Green which is worth

more than a glance. Here are some attractive old cottages leading down to the heath where cricket has been played since
1816. In that area was the nonconformist chapel which had
its origins in Milford in a building which had been, appropriately, a cattle shed. Some of the shed was used in the construction of the first chapel in 1860 and there was room for 60
people. Twelve years later an iron chapel was secured from
Alton, and at a total cost of £742 a new site and building
afforded room for 150 worshippers and, in an adjoining
schoolroom, 60 children.

Congregationalism continued to grow in the village and in
1902 the iron building was dwarfed by a new stone chapel
which accommodated 200 people and cost £1,200. Milford,
and its neighbour at Elstead, enjoyed happy times, but slowly
attendances declined and now only the chapel at Elstead
remains, while Milford's United Reformed Church members
are ministered to from Godalming.

🍁 MOLESEYS

These riverside urban areas face Hampton Court across the
Thames which in Henry VIII's time was crossed by ferry. A
wooden bridge went up in 1753 and was replaced by another
structure of wood 25 years later. In 1865 the river was
spanned by iron and then, in 1933, Lutyens and W.P.
Robinson, an engineer, built the present Hampton Court
Bridge. East Molesey was linked to the capital by train in
February 1849 and this transformed the district – fields and
orchards disappearing in favour of houses.

West Molesey has long had a sporting side. Archery, cricket, horse racing, golf, barefist boxing and even illicit duelling
have drawn large crowds to Molesey Hurst. Cricket was recorded there as early as 1731 and it is held that the first leg before

wicket decision was recorded there in 1775. In 1758 there was one of the country's earliest golf matches and in the early 1800s large bets were placed as prize fighters slugged it out for hours at a time. More recently Hurst Park racecourse was a popular venue for punters who came out from London. The course was laid in 1890 and lasted until 1962 when it was sold for housing development. Molesey's football ground at the Priory was the scene of an early balloon ascent in May 1785.

🍁 MUNSTEAD

Gertrude Jekyll is everywhere in West Surrey, but her presence is probably greatest here in this leafy appendage south of Godalming. Munstead House was built for her and her mother on open heath by J.J. Stevenson in 1877-78, and when Mrs Jekyll died in 1895 her son, Sir Herbert, took over the house, with Gertrude moving to Munstead Wood which Edwin Lutyens built for her. Earlier, when Mrs Jekyll was alive, Gertrude had commissioned Lutyens to build The Hut so that she could receive her friends.

Lutyens and Jekyll in West Surrey go together like milk and cream, the great gardener adding the topping to the fine designs. Lutyens was born in Thursley in 1869, knighted in 1918, and died in 1944. His architecture is universally known. He set up a London practice at the age of 19 and was consulting architect for the Hampstead Garden Suburb project in 1908, the joint architect for the building of New Delhi from 1913, designer of the Cenotaph in Whitehall in 1919, plus buildings such as the British Embassy in Washington, the Midland Bank in the City, and Grosvenor House in Park Lane. The Second World War prevented his designs for a Roman Catholic cathedral in Liverpool coming to fruition.

Gertrude Jekyll, who was born in 1843, lived at Munstead

Wood for 35 years. She had to forsake her first love of painting when her eyesight deteriorated, but this personal loss quickly became the gain of horticulturalists everywhere. Miss Jekyll encouraged the younger Lutyens in his work, and her skill was the perfect complement.

❧ MYTCHETT

Hitler's number two, Rudolf Hess, was held for 13 months in Mytchett Place before being tried for war crimes at Nuremburg. Hess had flown alone to Scotland in the spring of 1941 in a bizarre attempt to end the Second World War. His demands for a free Germany ended only in him being taken a prisoner and locked up in the Tower of London before being moved to Mytchett. An article in the *Surrey Advertiser* in 1974 gave a graphic description of Hess, who several times attempted suicide while at Mytchett. The house was surrounded by army camps and 'within this stronghold began the interrogation of one of history's oddities', the newspaper reported. 'A bizarre freak, he was examined and observed by psychiatric experts from all over the world.'

Mytchett Place, built in 1779 and greatly extended in Victorian times, was fortified in three days against possible commando attacks. 'Two detachments of Coldstream Guards and one of the Scots Guards were detailed to watch over Hess. Total security closed in around the bewildered fugitive. Even concealed microphones were installed to monitor anything he might say either awake or asleep. The interior of the building was wired up like a cage and Hess, who was known simply as Johnathan or J, was never left unattended.'

The newspaper baron, Lord Beaverbrook, visited Hess on behalf of Churchill and pronounced him sane, and in time he was taken to Nuremburg and sentenced to life in prison. Hess saw out his days in Spandau Prison in Berlin where, when he died a very old man, he was the only inmate and was watched night and day at great expense by a multi-national team of guards.

The Hess connection is the stuff of history, as is the Basingstoke Canal, of course. Except that the canal is living history, and in Mytchett there is an excellent visitor centre which tells the story of the waterway and is an ideal start and finish point for walkers and cyclists who wish to use the tow-path.

🍁 NEWCHAPEL

This is where the first European Church of Jesus Christ of Latter-Day Saints (the Mormons) was built in 1958 and where there is a visitor centre. Newchapel is south-west of Lingfield on a B road to Crawley, and it is where the head of the Pears Soap company once had a residence, Newchapel House, erected in 1908.

🍁 NEWDIGATE

This quiet, sleepy village down near the Sussex border was the first place in the county to have an iron works. It was in 1553 at Ewood to the north of the village that Christopher Darrell set up his foundry and was able to make use of a directive which allowed him to use trees on his land, whereas Elizabethan Acts prevented others from felling timber 'for making coles for the making of iron'.

There has always been a good quantity of wood around Newdigate, and many of the older houses have local oak in their construction. St Peter's church probably dates from the

13th century, and its dominant feature is its wooden tower and octagonal spire. The tower is supported by oak beams and it and the one at Burstow are the only all-wooden towers in the county.

The tower contains six bells 'of whose silvery notes the Newdigate men are justly proud', said an earlier writer. Bellringers from the village have been well known for decades. The Old Six Bells was a smugglers' haunt with underground passages, one of which was said to lead to the vicarage.

An early parson was George Steere, who was appointed by King James in 1610. He was given a school house and £6 13s 4d a year to teach four children. The school was in ruins in 1838 and a new building erected in 1872.

🍁 NORMANDY

Cobbett died here in 1835. The great politician spent his last days at Normandy Farm, but his body was taken back the few miles to Farnham, his birthplace, and buried in the family grave close to the main door of St Andrew's church in the town.

William Cobbett was born in Bridge Square, Farnham, at the public house which now bears his name, in 1762. He is best remembered for his *Rural Rides*, a collection of writings about his horseback journeys, many of them through Surrey. But Cobbett was also variously a gardener, lawyer's clerk, soldier, politician and farmer. He even served two years in jail for seditious libel for which he was also fined £1,000.

Guildford Races came to Normandy in the 1870s, long after the halcyon days of the turf on Merrow Downs and following an experiment on a track at Chilworth. But the event got a bad press in the *Surrey Advertiser* in an editorial under the heading 'The Perils of Sporting in Surrey'. The newspaper said: 'Greece

may be bad, but really Normandy (in England, we mean) on
Monday was worse, for gentlemen who went there fancied that
no military escort would be required. They were sadly mistak-
en. Quietly pinioned in open daylight, in the sight of hundreds,
they were relieved of valuable field glasses, or within a stone's
throw of a railway station, held while watches and money
were stolen, the bandits, with cool assurance, saying that
these were somewhat of the kind of thing they required.'

The editorial mentioned 'plunder, gambling and rowdyism'
at Normandy but ended by stating that 'racing is a perfectly
lawful sport, that it is patronised by the highest personages in
the land, and that so long as it occupies this position, those
who take part in it ought to have that protection which the law
guarantees to all persons in this country who may be engaged
in lawful pursuits'.

On the same page of the newspaper was a letter from someone who signed himself 'Promoter'. It claimed that the Chief of
the County Constabulary was 'neglect' as he was 'informed at
Scotland Yard that the county men were bound to protect the
public. I am indeed sorry to hear so many gentlemen were
robbed'.

Pigs were a problem for users of the commons back in the
1920s. They obstructed the footpaths and made them dirty,
and parish councillors won permission from the War Office to
erect stiles and gates to stop animals from leaving the commons, although the paths remained unfenced. There had been
swine in the area since time immemorial, on land from which
Henley Park evolved. Henley Park, a mansion built in the
1700s, was the headquarters of an engineering concern until
1983 when it was sold.

🍁 NORNEY

St Mary's church which stands at the crossroads at Norney is the work of the eminent architect, Sir George Gilbert Scott. It is the parish church of Shackleford but is isolated from the centre of the village. Scott was the son of a Buckinghamshire clergyman, and was born in 1811. His commissions, with his partner, William Bonython Moffatt, were thought to number at least 750, and included the Albert Memorial in Kensington Gardens, the Martyrs' Memorial at Oxford, Reading Gaol, the entrance to Dean's Yard at Westminster, restoration at Bath Abbey, the Home Office and Foreign Office in Whitehall, and St Pancras Station Hotel. So Shackleford's parish church and several others in the county were the creation of an architect whose work is known to everyone who visits the capital.

Sir George died in 1878 and his sons maintained the family's eminence. George Gilbert, the younger (1837-97), who was the eldest son, and John Oldrid (1841-1913), the second son, carved themselves reputations in the field of architecture. George Gilbert, the younger, was a Fellow of Jesus College, Cambridge, where he had an academic career of distinction. He was later in a partnership which produced church fittings of pre-Raphaelite design, and assisted his father and brother. He was the author in 1884 of the *History of English Church Architecture*, and editor of his father's book, *Personal and Professional Recollections*.

George Gilbert, the younger's second son, Giles Gilbert, who was knighted in the 1920s, won a competition in 1903 for the design of the Anglican Cathedral in Liverpool, and when he died in 1960 it was still to be completed. Locally, Sir Giles Gilbert Scott designed the War Memorial Chapel at Charterhouse School, Godalming, and in London his works included Battersea Power Station, Waterloo Bridge, and the rebuilding of the House of Commons.

The church at Norney is a mile from the centre of Shackleford village, but this little area just off the A3 has a community feel about it, no doubt brought on by the presence of the village hall and the junior school, a mellow Victorian building which gives the appearance of being a pleasant place to have one's elementary education, a contention supported, perhaps, by the standard of work displayed at exhibitions, including the annual Surrey County Show. The children at the 1984 show had the honour of singing for Princess Anne.

The lych gate at the church is to the memory of William Brodrick, the eighth Viscount Midleton of nearby Peper Harow, and on the war memorial on the opposite side of the road are the names of 24 men from Shackleford and Peper Harow who were killed in the First World War, and a further five, including Major the Hon M.V. Brodrick MC, Coldstream Guards, who did not return from the 1939-45 hostilities.

Phyllis Nicholson, the authoress, loved Norney during the 1930s and 1940s and wrote about the beauty of the place. It remains a rural corner in spite of the rush of traffic close by.

🍁 NUTFIELD

There is an industry as old as the Romans in this A25 village east of Redhill. The history of the village is bound up in the gathering of fuller's earth at sites to the north of the main road. Fuller's earth was first recorded in the Roman period and over the centuries has sustained many a Nutfield family.

Its original use was in the preparation of woollen and worsted cloth. Now, its properties have a wider application, such as in refining oil and in toilet preparations, and the earth is exported around the world. That was not the case in the reign of Edward II when export of the substance was prohibited.

The Domesday survey noted a church and a mill in Nutfield, but the present church dates from the 12th century. There were mills north and south of the village, and the southern one, King's Mill, was featured in a documentary film some years ago entitled *One hundred years of gearing.*

Four hundred years ago conditions were so tough that one man was given leave to attend a church other than Nutfield's because travelling was so difficult that he could not be at morning service, return home and be back for evening prayers as he was required to do. Permission was granted provided that the man attended Nutfield church four times a year to take Communion.

In Elizabeth I's time Martin Gummyns, a collier, of Nutfield, was sentenced to be hanged for burglary. He and others unknown stole a pair of sheets (worth 6s 8d), two shirts (6s), a smock (3s 4d), a cupboard cloth (6s), five rails (10s), five ker-chiefs (5s), and two ells of holland cloth (4s). Gummyns was sentenced at Croydon Assizes in 1579.

🍁 OAKWOODHILL

St John the Baptist is one of the remotest churches in the county. Deep down a lane which stops in the woods at the gate, it is reached only after a stiff climb up a path. A peaceful visit is assured, a sunny springtime afternoon, surrounded by the churchyard flowers, the blossom and the budding trees, being particularly memorable. The church, however, first built in 1390, will probably be locked. Do thieves and vandals really penetrate such places of worship so far off the beaten track in broad daylight? Should not a church offer a welcome rather than a bolted oak door?

🍁 OCKHAM

Nestling quietly to the east of the A3 and south of the M25, Ockham has long been dominated by its park which was bought by the first Lord King, who was Queen Anne's Lord Chancellor. It eventually passed into the hands of his descendants, the Lovelaces, whose name is perpetuated by a local ward on Guildford Borough Council.

The old semaphore station on Chatley Heath, near the village, is a monument now; more than 160 years ago it was a vital link in the chain which sent messages to and from the Admiralty in London to ships in the Channel. Chatley Heath was the point at which the unfinished branch line to Plymouth set off for Worplesdon, the Hog's Back and beyond. In those days wells on the local commons yielded deposits of Epsom salt.

This was the birthplace of William de Ockham who, before he died in 1349, engaged in controversies with Popes John XXII and Benedict XII.

In the churchyard, noted Manning and Bray, was the body of a very large oak, 12ft high and with the top broken off, and in the middle was a young oak. Also in the churchyard, a gravestone to a carpenter named Spong had a verse composed by Lord King, the Lord Chancellor, which went:

'Who many a sturdy oak had laid along,
Fell'd by death's surer hatchet, here lies Spong.
Posts oft he made, yet ne'er a place could get,
And liv'd by railing, tho' he was no wit.
Old saws he had, altho' no antiquarian;
And styles corrected, yet was no grammarian.
Long liv'd he Ockham's premier architect;
And lasting as his fame a tomb t'erect

In vain we seek an artist such as he,
Whose pales and gates were for eternity.
So here he rests from all life's toils and follies,
O spare awhile, kind Heav'n, his fellow labourer Hollis!'

Hollis was said to be the estate bricklayer.

🍁 OCKLEY

Red roses grow around some of the gravestones in St Margaret's churchyard – just as they did over 300 years ago when that great rambler, John Aubrey, came upon Ockley. 'Anciently the custom here for betrothed lovers was to plant rose trees at the head of the grave of a deceased lover, should either party die before the wedding. In the churchyard are many red rose trees planted among the graves which have been there beyond man's memory,' wrote Aubrey in the 17th century.

Today's roses are not the ones Aubrey saw, but there is the impression that little has changed in this corner of the parish. The village of Ockley lies on a straight section of the A29 and it is not surprising to discover that here was the road the Romans knew as Stone or Stane Street. It is as straight as a die, and through travellers are forced to miss the beauty of the place because of the constant speed the road affords.

There are four pubs along the road through the village and many old timbered cottages look out on to the cricket field on Ockley Green. Sportsmen have done battle for years alongside the A29, but go back more than 11 centuries and there was a battle of a different kind on Ockley Green and up the slopes of nearby Leith Hill. In AD 851, more than 200 years before the Battle of Hastings, the Danes were routed. The invaders swept

St Margaret's church, Ockley.

through Kent and down the Thames. Their target was Winchester, but they had not reckoned with Ethelwulf of Wessex. He marched up Stone Street from Chichester and faced the enemy 'hard by Ockley wood'. The battle was fierce and at the end there were few Danes left to tell the tale. 'Blood stood ankle deep' after the slaughter.

🍁 OLD WOKING

This was the original Woking and in the 17th century a market town. Henry VIII knew it for its Old Palace, as did Elizabeth I and James I, the latter giving Edward Zouch of Hoe Place the manor in 1620. Zouch was responsible for demolishing the palace, whose materials were spread around with the stained glass ending up at Sutton Place. In the grounds of Hoe Place was a brick tower from which a beacon was said to direct messengers to James I when he was staying with Zouch. A letter in the *Surrey Advertiser* in 1926 from Lord Onslow stated that the tower stood on land once owned by his father. His lordship understood the tower had been used as a beacon or telegraph station for naval signalling between London and Portsmouth, and that it was supposed to have been used in the fight against the Spanish Armada.

🍁 ONSLOW VILLAGE

One mile from Guildford's famous High Street setts, and looked down on by the cathedral, is this planned village which was established in the 1920s on land owned by Lord Onslow, grandfather of the present earl who lives in Clandon Park. The Onslow Village Association bought the land and over the years it kept a tight rein on the development of the area. In 1984, though, feelings were aroused and headlines made when the

association, in the face of Government policy on home owner-
ship and tenants' rights to buy, decided to dissolve and offered
the shareholding tenants their homes at considerably less than
the market value.

🍁 OTTERSHAW

Sir George Gilbert Scott's red-brick Christ Church is a striking
feature of this widespread village built on the heath between
Woking and Chertsey. Erected in 1864, it stands on a knoll
beside the main road with the rounded altar end in striking
contrast to the spire. Ottershaw does not appear in the
Domesday Book but long before the survey King Alfred's charter of AD 890 referred to land called Otreshagh which is
thought to be at this place.

Thomas Day, an 18th century writer of children's litera-
ture, lived at Anningsley Park and, according to a writer at the
turn of the century, he was a man 'whose life and character
occupy an extremely interesting chapter in the records of the
eccentricities of genius'. In the last eight years of his life from
1781 he 'took up farming energetically, lived simply without a
carriage, saw no society, and spent his income upon improving
his estate. He lost money by his farm, but was consoled by the
employment given to the poor. He declined invitations to take
part in political agitation, preferring his schemes of moral and
social reform, and approving of Pitt's administration. He studied mechanics, chemistry, and physic, became a good lawyer,
and wrote *Sandford and Merton* to set forth his ideal of manli-
ness.'

🍁 OUTWOOD

There will always be a steady stream of visitors to this hamlet because of its windmill. The place is off the beaten track but there is some good country round about, and the tiny cricket ground is picturesque. But it is the windmill that people come to see.

151

Those who went there before November 1960 saw two mills. The larger of the two, known as a smock mill because its shape resembled that of an old countryman's smock, collapsed of old age and now its former companion, a post mill, stands alone on its lofty site. It is said to be the oldest working mill in England, having been built in 1665-66 when, the story goes, the men working on it watched London burn.

🍁 OXSHOTT

Commuter land amid heaths, close to A3 and M25, railway station to Waterloo, pleasant towns of Leatherhead and Esher close by. Not the words of an estate agent but my description of Oxshott. Luxury homes abound in this urban village with its busy shopping centre. It has been known as Oakshott, Ockshot and Oxshot, and in its High Street around 1913 were found five sherds of Roman pottery. Bottles of Jessops Wells water at 6d each were said to contain a powerful potion from a well in woods near Fairoak Lane, Oxshott.

🍁 OXTED

The old village is a charming place but all around there has been development. In spite of the busy M25 just to the north, Oxted continues to be troubled by traffic because of the ongoing popularity of the A25 as an alternative to motorway travel. Barrow Green Court, the manor house, is 17th century and was once the home of the historian Grote. Close by is St Mary's church with its short 12th century tower. The Old Bell Inn is 15th century and a well known watering hole in East Surrey. Oxted's Master Park was a gift by Charles Hoskins Master, Lord of the Manor, in 1923: 'the greater part of the Marls Field as it is originally known laid out and preserved for ever thereafter for the healthy recreation and amusement of the inhabitants of the parish of Oxted and their friends'.

Walkers on the North Downs Way must negotiate a steep flight of man-made steps close to the tunnel, constructed in 1878, that takes the railway under the chalk escarpment. They would be fortunate indeed now to hear the sound of the nightingale whose quintessentially British song had, much earlier, been recorded for the gramophone by the BBC and had made Oxted's name well known around the world.

The village was in the news in 1997 following the death of Diana, Princess of Wales, when the body of her friend Dodi Fayed, who died with her in the road accident in Paris, was exhumed at Brookwood cemetery and reburied at the Oxted estate of his father, Mohamed Al Fayed, the owner of Harrods.

🍁 PEASLAKE

This is one of the county's most out of the way villages, tucked away on the slopes of Hurt Wood which was given to the public for 'air and exercise' in the 1920s. The Bray family of Shere, in whose parish Peaslake is situated, has quarried the local hillside for generations, and there are many properties built of Pitch Hill stone.

The church of St Mark was constructed of local sandstone and much of the carving was done by village craftsmen. It celebrated its centenary in 1989. The Romans were in Peaslake in the second century; the late Sir Adrian Boult had a home in the village in recent years; and there is a last resting place for Quakers in a special burial ground.

There is some fine walking and riding country and many visitors quench their thirst at the accommodating Hurtwood Inn.

🍁 PEASMARSH

A grizzly past is attached to this area in the parish of Shalford between Guildford and Godalming, for it was the place where public hangings were carried out. One, about 1820, saw men on the gallows after the murder of a farmer and theft of a side of bacon. One is said to have called to the other: 'Shall I ? Shall I?' This was thought to mean 'Shall I confess?' The other replied: 'No. Damn it, die like a man.'

Peasmarsh today comprises little more than a few houses, some industry and a crematorium. It lies between the river Wey and the main railway line between London and Portsmouth. It is not the place Cobbett would remember travelling through in 1882. 'Everybody that has been from Godalming to Guildford', he wrote, 'knows that there is hardly another such a pretty four miles in all England. The road is good; the soil is good; the houses are neat; the people are neat; the hills, the woods, the meadows, all are beautiful. Nothing wild and bold, to be sure; but exceedingly pretty, and it is almost impossible to ride along these four miles without feelings of pleasure, though you have rain for your companion, as it happened to be with me.'

Peasmarsh is still tolerably rural and the main cluster of houses are separated from the road by a wide expanse of common land. In the early years of the 20th century children swarmed to Peasmarsh Common to climb trees and watch the delivery carts being driven through the ponds to keep the wheels moist and prevent the nails from falling out. It is recorded that red-backed shrike once nested there. This is the now rare bird known as the butcher because it impales its prey on thorns or barbed wire. Perhaps its nesting location was apt in view of Peasmarsh's barbaric past.

🍁 PEPER HAROW

Peper Harow Park was the seat of the Lords Midleton of Cork from the early 1700s. The Midletons have left but the park remains much as it was. The present Grade I listed mansion was built in 1775 and, after a major fire a few years ago, has been restored and converted into apartments. It is south-east of the original house which was where the second Duke of Richmond (of Goodwood) was entertained while playing Alan Brodrick (Lord Midleton's son and heir) at cricket.

The ground on which they played is used today by the Peper Harow Cricket Club, and the 18th century gentlemen led their teams in games played to rules which were, in part, not dissimilar to our Laws of Cricket. On a visit to the park, and with but a touch of imagination, you can picture the scene. The rustic quality remains, albeit under the care of more modern machinery. There, too, are the Cedars of Lebanon which were planted as seedlings from pots in 1735.

Peper Harow appeared in the Domesday Book and the mill in 1086 could have been at Eashing just a little way downstream on the Wey. There are bridges almost as old in the park and, like others in the neighbourhood, they seem certain to have been constructed by the Cistercian monks from Waverley. On the edge of the parish is a popular riverside spot called Somerset Bridge. Again the Wey is crossed by a fine bridge, the middle arch being 700 years old, and it is on the site of the Saxon river crossing of Sumoeres forda. The highways authorities have, to their credit, refrained from adding an accompanying bridge as has happened elsewhere, notably upstream at Elstead and Tilford.

The Waverley monks farmed at Oxenford on the edge of Peper Harow Park on land that had been granted to their abbey in the early 12th century. The buildings at Oxenford are imitation 13th century. The fifth viscount employed Pugin to build a farm and gatehouse in 1844 in a style which bore resemblance to the grange which had been pulled down 69 years earlier. That leaves the pond close to the road as the most ancient relic at Oxenford.

Pugin also built an arch in the same style over nearby Bonfield Spring which, said Aubrey, cured sore eyes and ulcers. The historian also noted that 'near to this place, by digging for carrots (two spits deep) have been found gold and silver money, not Roman, but old English; as also rings...; which makes the inhabitants give 2s per acre more than elsewhere, in hopes of finding more'.

Graves of the Midletons are in the churchyard of St Nicholas near to the mansion. The little church was worked on by Pugin after one of its incumbents, the Rev Owen Manning, had become known as the compiler of much of a major history of the county. A much later vicar, the Rev William Shaw, was a noted natural historian who observed in 1925 that a thorn tree at the end of the church was 800 years old, and yew trees in the churchyard were 1,300 years old and would live as long again.

🍁 PIRBRIGHT

The heart of this attractive village is very green. There is a lot of open space in the centre where sport is played and children play. The village duck pond is overlooked by shops and the Cricketers pub which has an attractive sign depicting a scene from the game as it looked in the 18th century.

Pirbright is not entirely surrounded by military land but a large chunk of it is, and the two appear to get on. One suspects that the villagers have learned to live with the Army, so long have the soldiers been around. In 1911 it was recorded that three-quarters of the parish had been acquired by the War Office.

Church Lane leads not unnaturally to St Michael's which has a square, rather squat tower made, said one writer in the 19th century, with 'stones dug from the neighbouring commons'. The churchyard stretches back towards the village, and just inside the gate is the grave of Henry Morton Stanley, the man who uttered the immortal words: 'Dr Livingstone, I presume.' Stanley, an American journalist, talked his way into the history books in 1871 when, having been sent to Africa to look for Livingstone, he met the Scottish explorer beside Lake Tanganyika. Stanley was then 30 years old and he lived for another 33 years. He had requested that his body be buried beside that of Livingstone in Westminster Abbey but this was refused, and so his last resting place became a Surrey churchyard beneath a huge piece of Dartmoor granite – a British menhir, one writer called it – which dwarfs all the other memorials.

Back in 1802 Pirbright's vestry received the sum of 2s 6d from George III as a token of his majesty's gratitude after villagers had rescued him from a bog when his coach overturned on the outskirts of the settlement. Earlier still Pirbright had been the home of Admiral John Byron, an explorer and grandfather of the poet, who planted an avenue of Scots firs called Admiral's Walk which extended for a mile over Government land attached to the ranges.

Queen Victoria's diamond jubilee in 1897 was a great occasion in the village, with Lord and Lady Pirbright, of nearby Henley Park, treating all the residents to a fete on the green, making a number of presentations and giving a drinking fountain as a memorial. Two years later the village hall was built and in 1901 the recreation ground was given by the Pirbrights as a celebration of Edward VII's accession to the throne.

🍁 PIXHAM

A Lutyens church and a mill are two delights in this area
north-east of Dorking. St Martin's church was built in 1903
while the earliest date known for a mill at Pixham is 1595
although the present mill has an 1837 date. When it was put
up for sale at the end of the 19th century it was advertised as
'situate on a stream of water that never fails'. This was the
Pippbrook which rises on Leith Hill and flows a few miles to
enter the Mole at Pixham. The mill was working until the mid-
1920s and is now a private residence.

🍁 PUTTENHAM

There is an inscription on a gravestone in the cemetery which
reads: 'In their deaths they were not divided.' A quite ordinary
line, perhaps, but in the case of Albert and Annie Keen there is
an extraordinary story. These two country folk were the victims of a brutal double murder, and their killer was never
brought to justice.

The Keens lived in a simple cottage which bore their name
on common land in the south of the parish. They had lived
there since their marriage, and Albert was born there. His family had been the occupants for more than one hundred years.
Their lives had been quite unspectacular. Albert had worked
for several of the big houses round about, and was a farm foreman at the time of his death.

They died in October 1932; Annie in the scullery of their
home, and Albert on the way home, his body being found in nearby Cutt Mill Pond. A massive police operation led to the arrest of a
man with local connections, but after a trial at Surrey Assizes at
Kingston he was acquitted.

Albert and Annie Keen were buried in a grave next to his parents, and more than 65 years later their story is remembered only by older residents of the district.

The ponds at Cutt Mill are hauntingly beautiful. Six in all, they are known by their collective name but accurately should be referred to as Cutt Mill, The Tarn, Warren, General's, Long and Trout. The Tarn is the one beloved of walkers and anglers.

Puttenham's church nestles at one end of the village street, and there was once a spire on top of the tower, but this was destroyed by a fire in 1736 which started in the blacksmith's forge. Water for the village was taken from a well just inside the church gate until the mid-1700s when the source was filled in. Then, on Palm Sunday in 1972, churchgoers were surprised to see a very pleasant cypress tree drop through the ground. The village well, which few knew about, had reappeared. Behind the church is Puttenham Priory, a large residence which was once owned by the founder of *Picture Post* magazine. Built in 1762, the Priory was bought from Sir Edward Hulton by Guildford Hospital Management Committee in 1950 and, for 26 years until it was sold, was an old people's home.

Henry Beedell and his son, also Henry, were successive rectors for 96 years, while another Puttenham priest was Charles Kerry whose work as an archaeologist and local historian is still referred to. The Kerry manuscripts record many interesting stories, including a nice piece of folklore about the siting of the church in Puttenham. According to Kerry, the church was to be on Church Croft Knob in a plantation well out of the village on the way to Cutt Mill. But the pious intentions of the builders, Kerry was told, were frustrated by fairies who removed by night what had been erected in the day to the place were the church now stands. Church Croft continues to appear on maps.

Puttenham, sheltered on the south side of the Hog's Back,

is a popular village close enough to the county town for convenience but still with a rural identity. Its golf course stretches over the heath where Queen Victoria reviewed the Surrey Rifle Volunteers in 1851. Puttenham was until quite recently the eastern limit of the Alton and Farnham hop fields, and was, on Bowen's map of 1749, 'noted for its pleasant and healthy situation'. Bowen, more than two centuries on, could probably make that claim today.

🍁 PYRFORD

The old church of St Nicholas looks across to the ruined Newark Priory from its position above the Wey, but since 1966 there is no longer a view of Newark Mill. The building, said Jack Hillier in his 1950s book, *Old Surrey Watermills*, must take pride of place among such structures in Surrey. It was one of the few generally known outside the county. Sadly, it was burned down in the 1960s.

Elizabeth I was a visitor to Pyrford when a secretary, Sir John Wolley, and his wife, who was a member of the More family of Loseley and a lady-in-waiting to the Queen, lived at Pyrford Place. The estate was bought by Denzil Onslow in 1677 but the house was demolished 100 years later by Robert Onslow. John Aubrey has left us with the following record of a visit on 23 August 1681: '...there was much company, and such an extraordinary feast, as I had hardly seen at any country gentleman's table. What made it more remarkable was that there was not anything save what his (Denzil Onslow) estate about it affords; as venison, rabbits, hares, pheasants, partridges, pigeons, quails, poultry, all sorts of fowl in season from his own decoy near his house, and all sorts of fresh fish. After dinner, we went to see sport at the decoy, where I never saw so many herons. The seat stands in a flat, the ground pasture

By
Pyrford Lock

rarely watered and exceedingly improved since Mr Onslow bought it. The house is timber, but commodious, with one ample dining room.'

The parish shares its living with Wisley and has been known as Pyrford-cum-Wisley. The incumbent through both World Wars was the Rev Cuthbert Hamilton who moved in 1913 from Farnham, where he had been a curate for three years and a more than useful batsman in Farnham's cricket team.

🍁 RIPLEY

Cricket and cycling made Ripley famous in the 19th century. One took place on the Green behind the main road, the other centred around the gabled and low ceilinged Anchor Inn. Ripley, 25 miles from the centre of London before modern roads shrunk the distance, was the ideal halfway stop for early cyclists as the sport began to take a hold in the south.

The first riders came to the village in 1870 and the Dibble sisters, Annie and Harriet, welcomed them to their hostelry. They made such a fuss of them that in any one year almost 7,000 cyclists, mounted on penny-farthings or boneshakers, signed the visitors' book at the Anchor where Annie Dibble, like her sister a devout churchgoer, was known to read the Bible to her guests.

When these two ladies died – Annie in July 1895 and Harriet in October the following year – cyclists clubbed together and had a stained glass window to their memory installed in the south aisle of St Mary's church in the village.

Ripley cricketers have been active for more than two centuries. In 1749 they combined with players from Richmond to play London, and two years later they joined forces with Thursley cricketers to meet the Gentlemen of Eton. Ripley Green was the venue of a match between Chertsey and the rest of Surrey in 1762 when an ordinary (meal) was supplied by Mr Fowler's White Horse. Surrey played Middlesex there in 1763; and 22 of Surrey challenged England at Ripley in 1802. The village also joined with Cobham, Woking and Pirbright to play two matches against the five-year-old Farnham club in 1787. Farnham were asked to exclude their best bowler in the first fixture, in spite of the already unbalanced nature of the side, but still won by seven wickets. The return, at Ripley, went to the home side by 101 runs.

Cricket is still played in the village, and cyclists continue to call but the days of the Dibbles are long gone. Ripley High Street, alas, has been troubled by traffic for too many years, in spite of a bypass being constructed, but the Anchor continues to be a popular hostelry. The Talbot Hotel, where Nelson often stopped, is nearby.

🍁 ROWLEDGE

The parish church of St James in Rowledge is in Hampshire. So, too, is the village school. A big hitter on the cricket field can hit the ball into the next county. The church is on the edge of Alice Holt Forest, which is wholly in Hampshire and has provided Rowledge men with work over the centuries.

Rowledge has grown considerably in recent years but still retains village charm. The square with its shops and public house, the Hare and Hounds, has always been a meeting place. Nearby, High Street gives the impression of hustle and bustle but it is just a residential road which once contained some handy shops.

Surrey ends and Hampshire begins in Fuller's Road which takes its name from one Nestor Fuller who, more than 100 years ago, came to Frensham Hill, a large house on the outskirts of the village and now renamed Frensham Heights School. The brewing family Charrington occupied Frensham Hill in the early part of the 20th century and the beautiful cricket ground in front of the house was the scene of some memorable matches. Cricket week at Frensham Hill was an annual occasion not to be missed, and local folk helped cater for such famous teams as MCC, Free Foresters and I Zingari.

During the First World War, Frensham Hill was a military hospital and scenes from there appear on old picture postcards which crop up frequently on the stalls run by dealers at local markets and fairs.

There has always been a strong cricket tradition in Rowledge and district. Just outside the village, in Hampshire, is the hamlet of Holt Pound where Surrey twice defeated England in the early 1800s. Rowledge cricketers used that same oval, made by William 'Silver Billy' Beldham in 1791 – its name was taken up by Surrey County Cricket Club when it moved to Kennington in 1845 – until their recreation ground was prepared. The village club dominated the local I'Anson Cup league in the 1980s, before leaving for pastures new. In 1985 it became the champion village side of England, and played at Lord's where it lost a nail-biting final to the Scottish champions.

Mike Hawthorn, Britain's first world motor racing champion, lived in Rowledge and was a colourful character in the district. Hawthorn, who won the title in 1958, lived life to the full but it lasted just short of 30 years, for the dashing bow-tied driver died at the wheel of a Jaguar in an accident on the Guildford bypass on 22 January 1959. He was a boyhood hero and I well remember him telling an assembly at Farnham Grammar School shortly before he died how he had won the world championship. His funeral service and procession stopped Farnham in its tracks and the wreaths and floral tributes at his graveside were from the legends and the elite of world motor racing. His gravestone in the town's cemetery depicts a racing car surrounded by a laurel wreath under which is the inscription 'A gay gallant sportsman'. Hawthorn's TT Garage in East Street, Farnham, was a mecca for boys who would press their noses against the plate glass and look at the gleaming racing cars and, hopefully, catch a glimpse of their idol. His death was a stunning blow to boys of my age who were beginning to tinker with old cars, and as keenly felt as the air crash at Munich the previous year which had robbed us of our favourite 'Busby Babes'.

🍁 ROWLY

An extension of Cranleigh on the road to Shamley Green but there is a sense of separation from its larger neighbour. It retains a post office, which is more than can be said of so many of our villages.

🍁 RUNFOLD

When driving along the old A31 at Runfold you barely notice a property called Barfield. It is a school and is back from the road on the junction of the lane to Crooksbury Hill. Few drivers would know of the significance of that spot, anyway. The name of John Henry Knight means little to most passers-by. But to those who know their motoring history J.H. Knight is recalled as a pioneer. Five years before the dawn of the 20th century Knight invented the first two-seater car and it was made in nearby Farnham.

Knight lived at Barfield, and the dusty, rutted roads round about were his test bed. He and his machines were a familiar sight in the district, preceded by a man carrying a red flag. His 1895 invention was capable of eight miles an hour and put the life of the flag carrier in peril, and at least on one occasion earned Knight a fine in the local magistrates' court.

Farnham was, and still is, rightly proud of him, and present-day Runfold has, it seems, been content to let its big brother have the glory.

Runfold, once in the centre of hop fields, is now a place to be passed through with barely a sideways glance, but to the south there is some delightful country dominated by Crooksbury Hill, first topped by pine trees more than 200 years ago. Those conifers have been a landmark for generations, in spite of being decimated during the Great War, but now a mast stands out more prominently on the skyline, albeit on an adjoining hill.

Crooksbury House was Lutyens's first country house in 1890. He designed it for Arthur Chapman and within a few years he was enlarging it. Later there was some additional work when Gertrude Jekyll added her influence in the garden.

The North Downs Way passes through Runfold, soon after its starting point at Farnham and shortly after leaving Moor Park.

🍁 RUSHMOOR

This is an outpost of the civil parish of Frensham and ecclesiastical parish of Churt and lies between Hankley and Churt commons. The road through Rushmoor is known locally as the 'Straight Mile' and it leads to the Pride of the Valley which was once one of the most rural of wayside public houses.

Across the road from the inn a path leads to the top of one of three conical hills known as the Devil's Jumps. Two are on private property, but Stony Jump is owned by the National Trust and affords a panoramic view through 360 degrees. The large outcrop of sandstone gives the hill its name but how did the Jumps become linked with the devil? Two legends have stood the test of time. One has the devil leaping from hill to hill while fleeing from Mother Ludlam at Waverley, coming to rest on nearby Kettlebury Hill before disappearing into Heccombe Bottom which is known now as the Devil's Punch Bowl. The other has the devil jumping from hill to hill and being knocked out with a stone thrown by Thor the god of thunder whose name is perpetuated in the neighbouring village of Thursley.

The Devil's Jumps have even been discussed in the House of Lords. In the 1920s their lordships were critical of the way the heather was being burnt and replaced with trees. Sheer vandalism, they claimed, but the Forestry Commission reported that it was providing jobs in a depressed area and, anyway, when the trees matured the beauty of the area would be enhanced. How right it was, but you have got to stand on the top of Stony Jump to agree. Try it at sunset on a summer's day or, if you want exhilaration, be there when a strong wind is blowing.

SALFORDS

A 'sad example of ribbon development' is one comment levelled at this village on the A23 south of Redhill. It is a fair description. Salfords, years ago, was quite rural, but the developers, both domestic and industrial, moved in and changed the face of the place. The parish council boundary takes in Sidlow to the west and here there is still green countryside. The Sal brook runs through Salfords and enters the Mole near Sidlow. Once it supplied water for a mill which twice burnt down before being converted into a guest house to cater for the demand brought about by the increase of traffic on the main road to Brighton on which, until 1881, there was a toll bridge. Salfords church of Christ the King is modern and was built by voluntary labour.

✹ SANDHILLS

A century or so ago the artist Graham Robertson called Sandhills a 'most unsophisticated little village' in 'the real English countryside'. Robertson, who was also a playwright, had moved into the house in which had lived Helen Allingham, whose paintings of Surrey are a delight to the eye. Mrs Allingham, a doctor's daughter from Burton-on-Trent, was born in 1848 and after her father died in 1862 the family moved to Birmingham where she studied art. She went on to the Royal Academy in London as one of the first intake of women students. Helen married the poet William Allingham in 1874 and the following year they moved to Sandhills. For the next 13 years, working in watercolours, she captured many delightful Surrey scenes which are now sold at auction at what the trade calls keen prices. She was a member of the Royal Society of Painters in Watercolours. Mrs Allingham moved back to London in 1888 but returned to Surrey and died at Haslemere in 1926.

The area, situated between Brook and Wormley, and close to Witley station, attracted other residents of note, including the artist Myles Birket Foster and the writer George Eliot, the pseudonym of Marian, or Mary Ann, Evans, who also lived at Shottermill, where she wrote part of *Middlemarch*. She and her common-law husband, fellow author George Lewes, lived briefly at Sandhills before returning to London where Lewes died in 1878. Two years later she married and again moved to Sandhills, but in December of that year she died suddenly.

🍁 SANDS, THE

Seale and The Sands go together like salt and pepper, but it is possible to have one without the other. The Sands is more off the beaten track than Seale, but there is a shop and a pub and a bowling club, not to mention Farnham Golf Club. It is also a place much favoured by motorists attempting shortcuts or trying to avoid traffic snarl-ups on the A31 or Blackwater Valley Road which are close by.

At weekends it is a favourite haunt of walkers, who can slake their thirst and find a good menu at the Barley Mow. The North Downs Way, which starts its journey quite unpromisingly at Farnham railway station before heading through soft woodland, bypasses The Sands as it crosses the golf course, but walkers need only detour a couple of hundred yards before finding sanctuary at the pub.

Crooksbury Hill, where Cobbett caught magpies in his youth, is no longer a prominent landmark after fir trees on its summit were either felled or were victims of high winds. But its location can still be determined because of the radio mast standing on neighbouring high ground. This tower has been in place for some years and whatever fuss was made about its siting in sensitive countryside has long since subsided. One supposes that the critical comment that has accompanied the increase in the number of telecommunications masts in the last few years will also subside as time passes.

🍁 SEALE

The roof tops of Seale can just be spotted through the trees on the drive over the Hog's Back between Farnham and Guildford. North of the ridge is the urban sprawl of Aldershot and district, while south, which is where Seale lies, is rural, agricultural land, pockmarked here and there by gravel and sand pits.

Seale, which has lost its shop, post office and school in recent times, has pleasant old cottages clustered near the church. In 1788 at Hampton Lodge came Noble, the Derby winner of two years earlier, to stand at stud. A fee of two guineas and half a crown to the groom was fixed but Noble, in spite of his success at Epsom, was a failure at Seale.

In Elizabeth I's time a farmer from the hamlet went to the gallows for theft. Nicholas Grauntham appeared at Croydon Assizes on 12 January 1575, charged with the theft at Guildford of a purse, worth fourpence, which contained four shillings in money, a gold ring valued at a guinea, and a silver ring worth 16d.

Up on the ridge the Hog's Back Hotel was formerly a house on the site of a semaphore station, known as Poyle Hill, which was on the London to Plymouth line abandoned before completion in 1830.

St Lawrence's church is mostly Victorian on the site of a 13th century church built at the expense of Waverley Abbey. Among the memorials is one in the north transept to Edward

Long, who perished in 1809 when the ship in which his regiment was sailing to Spain was sunk by a man-of-war in an accident. A school friend was responsible for erecting the tablet at Seale.

Between Seale and Elstead is Littleworth Cross where the architect Edwin Lutyens met the gardener Gertrude Jekyll for the first time. Lutyens designed a house called Squirrel Hill and it was in the garden of the famous rhododendron grower Harry Mangles that architect and gardener came together for a meeting that was to be the start of a great partnership. Across the road from that garden was, and still is, Littleworth Cross, a half-timbered house which may have been designed by Norman Shaw and contains some work by Lutyens.

🍁 SEND

Parish registers for the 18th century show just how strong the military presence was in Send. For 12 years from 1750 there was a camp on Send Heath and the records list many births,

Newark Priory, Send.

170

marriages and deaths of soldiers and their families. The men and their uniforms won the hearts of many a local girl. In 1759, 25 soldiers were married in the church of St Mary the Virgin; 14 went to the altar the following year; and 19 in 1761.

Three centuries earlier soldiers were involved in a skirmish in the area. On 14 June 1497, Cornish rebels marching on Kent reached Guildford and clashed with the outposts of the royal troops on the road to London. Old maps mark the spot where the road crossed the stream which joins the Wey near Send as St Thomas's Waterings.

The ruins of Newark Priory stand beside the river. It was founded by Ruald de Calva and his wife, Beatrice of Send, at the end of the 12th century, and was for the Augustinian order.

One of cricket's early giants, Edward Stevens, came from Send. Known as 'Lumpy' because of his size – or was it that he once ate an apple pie whole? – he was a member of the great Hambledon (Hampshire) club towards the end of the 18th century. His last match was for England against Hampshire in 1789 when he was 54. Thirty years later, on 7 September 1819, he died and was buried in the churchyard at Walton-on-

Send church.

Thames where he had lived and worked as gardener to a great cricket supporter and twice Postmaster General, the Earl of Tankerville.

'Lumpy' was as good a bowler as there was and it was through his misfortune that a third stump was introduced. Until 1775 the wickets were of two stumps and many a straight delivery, having been missed by the batsman, went clean through the gap. It happened to 'Lumpy' on three occasions when he was bowling to the last man in a match between five of Hambledon and five of All England at the Artillery Ground in London. He got his man in the end and Hambledon won the game, but afterwards it was considered 'not cricket' that a bowler should suffer so badly, and a middle stump was there and then brought in.

🍁 SHACKLEFORD

There is a lovely wooded lane in Shackleford where there are the remains of a lime kiln, long since disused. It had always fascinated me, but not until I read Gertrude Jekyll's explanation of the working of such a kiln did I have an understanding of its importance.

Miss Jekyll in *Old West Surrey* wrote that wagons brought chalk from a pit to the kilns which were 'built in steeply sloping ground by or near a roadside, where the loads of chalk could be drawn up to their top level. They are interesting wayside objects, and some of them that have been overgrown with brushwood, or that stand in what has become woodland, grown up during the 60 years or more that have passed since they were used, have an air of mystery that still brings back to me the thrill of fearful joy that they excited in my childish mind'.

The larger blocks of chalk, said Miss Jekyll, were built up

inside the kiln (which was circular in plan and open at the top), in the form of a rough arch...and the smaller pieces of chalk were filled in above. The space underneath was crammed with furze faggots, and a certain amount of burning converted the chalk into lime.

During the 1980s, the kiln was partially restored, but now, alas, it has been all but lost again beneath a jungle of what Gertrude Jekyll would have called brushwood.

Shackleford has some interesting old cottages grouped around the village shop and there is an unusual wavy wall in one garden. Richard Wyatt, the son of a Sussex parson, was the squire more than three centuries ago. He lived at Hall Place which in Henry VIII's time belonged to William de Shackleford. Hall Place was pulled down in 1797 and the land was added to nearby Peper Harow Park, but a new mansion was built in the 19th century and is now a preparatory school.

The church and school are apart from the village. St Mary's, designed by the eminent architect Sir George Gilbert Scott in 1865 stands proud on a crossroads opposite the war memorial in the area known as Norney and beloved of the authoress, Phyllis Nicholson, during the thirties and forties.

The narrow lane to Puttenham runs past Lydling where there is a farmhouse dating from about 1700 and where the Stovold family have farmed for centuries. Cross Farm has some Lutyens barns which have been converted into homes. The pond by the roadside at Lydling is home to ducks, coots and moorhens. A footpath leads to Rodsall which was Redessolha in the Domesday Book. The Bishop of Bayeux held Rodsall at the time of the survey. Tovi held it before 1066 and 'could go with it where he would. Then it answered for five hides; now for nothing'. There was land for two ploughs, and there were three villagers and four cottagers with one plough. There were two acres of meadow and woodland with four pigs. The value before 1066 and at Domesday was 40s.

🍁 SHALFORD

The Tillingbourne runs its course in this village just outside Guildford, and enters the Wey behind the church. Shalford suffers badly from being on the main road to Horsham, but there is enough charm off the beaten track to keep the visitor entertained.

It is a pleasant spot just a mile from the county town and popular with visitors because of the proximity of the Wey Navigation and its feeling of being in the countryside, in spite of the presence of a number of high tech office buildings.

There are some pleasant walks around the village which was once an important landing stage when barges plied the Wey. Gunpowder from the Chilworth mills was brought the short distance to the river bank and transferred for the waterborne trip to the capital. Now, pleasure craft use the river which is navigable as far upstream as Godalming.

Narrow boat cruises from Guildford Boat House travel upstream through St Catherine's Lock to Shalford where, at the junction of the Navigation with the old Wey and Arun

Former gunpowder store at Broadford Bridge, Shalford.

Canal – the so-called lost route to the sea – the river is wide enough to enable craft to turn around.

There were three mills in Shalford at the time of Domesday; there is one today. Shalford Mill, not too far from the church, was given to the National Trust in 1932. It was once the property of Major Arthur Godwin-Austen whose family is remembered on tablets in St Mary's church, an 1846 building on the site of the Domesday church. One of the Godwin-Austens explored and surveyed the north-west Himalayas.

The church end of the village is full of old houses and cottages, and the stocks are retained if somewhat dilapidated outside the churchyard wall.

🍁 SHAMLEY GREEN

The Romans were in Shamley Green, which is not surprising in view of its proximity to the temple at Farley Heath. In 1900 a cinerary urn was discovered at nearby Blackheath, where today you can find good hospitality at the Villagers public house; in the 1920s a coin was dug up when a well was being sunk at Green Lane Farm, and was identified as coming from Cyprus under Roman rule about AD 139; and as recently as 1970 a Romano-British burial urn was unearthed one foot below the surface when a post hole was being dug in Green Lane, and this contained cremated bones.

Shamley Green is a picturesque hamlet between Guildford and Cranleigh, with a charter for an annual fair granted by Oliver Cromwell to 'Shamble Lea'. Shops and houses are grouped around the green where cricket is played every summer weekend.

A tradition at Christ Church has it that when a funeral service is held a penny must be placed on the gatepost as the corpse is carried through the churchyard or a right of way will be established. The Congregationalists had a chapel built in 1836 but when interest declined the Strict Baptists moved in. Later, both denominations shared the building which eventually became so dilapidated that a new chapel was erected at the turn of the century.

🍁 SHEPPERTON

Film studios have sent the name of Shepperton around the world, provided you read the small print as the credits roll. They have given the place a certain prosperity and brought a lot of famous names to the area. Shepperton is on the Thames and came into Surrey in the 1970s. The church of St Nicholas dominates the centre and was built with masonry from an earlier church which was demolished when the river undermined its foundations. A medieval rector was William Grocyn (1504-13) who was one of the first teachers of Greek at Oxford and a friend of Erasmus who occasionally visited him at the Rectory. Other guests at the Rectory have included Richard III, who was said to have stayed there before the Battle of Bosworth Field, and the novelist George Eliot, who had connections elsewhere in Surrey, notably at Shottermill and Sandhills.

William Lindsay MP, who became lord of the manor in the second half of the 19th century, is credited with achieving much for Shepperton. He transformed the lives of many residents who until his appearance on the scene were existing in one-room cottages. Lindsay also financed much of the building of the railway branch line from Twickenham which reached Shepperton and Sunbury in 1864.

In a district where one place merges with another, Shepperton's neighbour in one direction is Lower Halliford where, it is held, a weeping willow in the garden of the poet Thomas Love Peacock grew from a cutting sent to him from St Helena when Napoleon was exiled on that South Atlantic island.

🍁 SHERE

Shere is the brightest jewel in the Tillingbourne valley's crown. The little river gurgles its way through the village where visitors and residents alike can sit on the banks and watch the ducks – descendants of those in Eric Parker's day. Since a bypass was built to the north in the 1960s, Shere has regained much of its calm. Overhanging buildings along the old A25 are no longer subjected to day and night traffic abuse. Visitors can look in peace – well, at certain times. Shere is packed to overflowing on fine weekends.

The village is the home of the Brays, a deep-rooted Surrey family whose members are remembered in St James's church. It was William Bray who completed the massive *History of*

The old ford, Shere.

Surrey begun by the Rev Owen Manning of Peper Harow, and whose volumes are much used by today's researchers. Manning died in 1801 and Bray, at the age of 65, took it upon himself to see that the work was finished. He visited every church and parish, and local historians will for ever be in his debt. He died in 1832 when aged 96.

The village rightly takes great pride in its appearance, and the church is no exception. There have always been parishioners keen and willing to look after the church, which was recorded in the Domesday Book, and there is a portrait of one of them in the porch. Emma Diggins, who died in 1907, is shown unlocking the door, and the caption reads: 'Faithful servant of the church.'

Christine the Anchoress, the daughter of Edward the Carpenter, caused a stir in the village back in 1329. She wanted to carry chastity and godly obedience to an extreme difficult to imagine in today's increasing secular society. And she got her way when the Bishop of Winchester gave his permission for her to be incarcerated in a cell barely large enough to take her small frame. Her only contact with the outside world was a squint and an aperture through which food was passed. She remained in situ, as it were, for three years until she decided that she needed a break. The Bishop eventually consented and Christine emerged into the sunlight, but later she returned to her self-imposed captivity, there probably to die, although the outcome is not recorded.

Shere attracts painters which is not unnatural for a village that has been named the 'home of art' and where one house was, at different times, the home of three Royal Acadamicians – Gilbett, Holl and Boehm. Smuggling and sheep stealing have also had a home in Shere and so, too, has the cloth trade. It was John Aubrey who said that the Old Parsonage House had been built upon 'woolsacks' or from the proceeds of the wool trade of the 17th century.

There is a brass in the church to Lord Audley whose son James was beheaded at Tower Hill for being a leader of the Cornish rebellion in 1497. James led his men through Shere on their way to Blackheath in Kent.

❧ SHOTTERMILL

Shottermill tends to be lumped on to Haslemere, but it deserves to be treated and looked at separately. Bordered by West Sussex and Hampshire, Shottermill tucks itself away under the hills of Hindhead and Blackdown. It has many picturesque corners, although one, the ponds, is just in West Sussex. The county boundary is the stream which runs through one of the parish's five mill sites, just below the London to Portsmouth railway line. To return to the ponds for a moment, they are two-tiered and were restored in 1955 as a memorial to the founders of the Haslemere Preservation Society, and are now owned by the National Trust.

The Trust, in fact, owns much land in Shottermill, whose ecclesiastical parish stretches up to the A3 at Hindhead and over the main road to the Hampshire border at Grayshott. Shottermill was in Frensham parish until the 1920s and was properly known as the tithing of Pitfold. Nowadays Pitfold is a quiet area off the A3 at the summit of the fearsomely steep Glen Lea, a narrow hill with a gradient of one in four which has tested cyclists for decades.

A reminder of Frensham control over the area is the property known as Frensham Hall close to a series of ponds from where the pioneering Surrey Trout Farm supplied the catch of many fishermen on rivers and streams throughout the land. Frensham Hall was the home of the well-known Baker family and by all accounts Edward Baker was none too popular back in the middle of the 19th century. One day as he rode home he discovered a trench had been dug across his path. And as he spurred his horse to jump the chasm a shot rang out and peppered his backside. Edward was determined that his 'exits and his entrances' would be carried out in safety so he built a lodge near the spot where the drive joined the highway to Hindhead.

Another story about Edward concerned his pack of hounds. When his estate was being sold to pay off his creditors, he arranged for his huntsman, on hearing the hound pack's lot number called, to sound a blast on his horn and yell. The hounds disappeared as they had been trained to do.

Here at Shottermill, on the road down from St Stephen's church to the county boundary, George Eliot resided for a short time and wrote much of *Middlemarch.*

🍁 SMALLFIELD

The largely modern village of Smallfield to the east of the M23 owes its origins to the wars with France many centuries ago. It was in the reign of Edward III that the estate of Smallfield Place was given to John de Burstow by Lord Burghersh as an acknowledgement of the assistance he gave when his lordship was thrown from his horse in battle. The Bysshe family were later owners and Edward Bysshe extended the house. He was a bencher of Lincoln's Inn in the reign of James I. Bysshe's father had been MP for Bletchingley during the 1620s and in 1640, and Bysshe himself was a member for Gatton in Cromwell's first Parliament in 1654 and in Richard Cromwell's Parliament five years later.

🍁 STANWELL

The name of this former Middlesex village is known to rose growers because in 1838 a hitherto unknown species was discovered in a local garden and given the name of Stanwell Perpetual. Two of the oldest buildings in the Spelthorne borough are in Stanwell: St Mary's church and Lord Knyvett's School. The church at the end of the green has a beautiful spire which was added to the tower in the 14th century. There are monuments to Lord and Lady Knyvett who both died in 1622 and an arcade of eight seats, now used by the choir, which were thought to have been made for the monks of Chertsey Abbey and given to Stanwell in 1415.

Lord Knyvett's School was built in 1624 to educate 'male children'. Sir Thomas (later Lord) Knyvett was the man who arrested Guy Fawkes and he was granted the manor of Stanwell in 1603 and, 10 years later, the manor of Staines. One of the last owners of Stanwell Place before it was demolished was Sir John Gibson who was instrumental in the design of the Mulberry Harbours which played such an important part in the success of the D-Day landings on the Normandy coast during the Second World War. Those constructions were towed across the Channel and placed in position off the French coast at Arromanches, where their remains can still be seen today.

🍁 STOKE D'ABERNON

Not too many people would put this village on the Mole on their honeymoon list, but William the Marshall did in 1189 and started a trend. William, or Guillaume le Marechal, and his bride, who was the heiress to the Earl of Pembroke, were offered Stoke Manor for the first honeymoon on record.

Stoke's church of St Mary the Virgin is the oldest in the county. It was built around AD 650 but only the south wall from that period exists today. The restoration has been described as both 'merciless' and 'wicked'. Inside are the oldest monumental brasses in the country – those of the d'Abernon knights. A brass of a knight in chain armour dated 1277 is of Sir John d'Abernon and is lifesize.

Sir John was Sheriff of Sussex and Surrey but in 1265 he

got himself embroiled in a spot of bother which led to him having to pay out about £600. The trouble started when a William
Hod of Normandy shipped to Portsmouth ten hogshead of
woad. Robbers stole it and took it to Guildford. Hod set off in
hot pursuit and seized back the woad and made it secure in
Guildford Castle. But then events took a horrible twist as a
counter-demand for the woad came from France and Sir John
d'Abernon became involved, it seems, right up to his neck.
There was a threat to burn down the castle, and even the
town, and Hod took proceedings against Sir John and won
after the under-sheriff had given in to the fresh demand. Sir
John was ordered to hand over six score marks.

Stoke d'Abernon, whose church is one of only five on the banks
of the Mole – Horley, Betchworth, Leatherhead and Cobham are
the others – was 'Stoche' in the Domesday Book and the rather
grand appendage was added when the d'Abernon family were
presented with the demesne. Elizabeth I stayed at the manor and
the records show it was there she knighted Thomas Vincent, who
was related to the d'Abernons.

🍁 SUNBURY

The racecourse at Kempton Park means a steady flow of visitors to Sunbury. Kempton Park was enclosed in 1246 and kept
stocked with deer until 1835. It has been used for horse racing
for 100 years or so. St Mary's church, built in 1752 on the site
of a 14th century building, was designed by the clerk of works
at Hampton Court. Sunbury Court, which is now used as a
youth centre by the Salvation Army, was erected in 1770. To
the west is the hamlet of Charlton with the delightful thatched
roof 16th century Harrow inn.

🍁 SUTTON GREEN

One house dominates this area near Guildford: Sutton Place. Built in the 1520s, it has been described as the best Tudor house in the South of England. Sir Richard Weston was granted the estate in 1521 after attending Henry VIII at the Field of the Cloth of Gold.

Weston, who built the house, was close to the King and remained so in spite of the fact that the monarch had Weston's son executed for suspicion of an affair with Anne Boleyn. That was in 1536, three years after Henry VIII visited Sutton Place. Weston's grandson, Sir Henry, became the heir to the estate and entertained Elizabeth I there for three days in 1591.

In 1613 the house and grounds came into the hands of another Sir Richard Weston who is remembered as the man who introduced canals to this country. He used a system he had seen in operation on the Continent to transform the river Wey between Guildford and Weybridge. Part of his inheritance was the village of West Clandon which he sold to Sir Richard Onslow in 1641. Weston the canal builder, who also brought the clover plant to this country, died in 1652 and his son carried on his work and ensured that the Wey Navigation opened the following year.

The Wey was made navigable by Acts of Parliament in Charles II's reign. The work of building 12 locks and digging 10 miles of channel had cost Weston £15,000. In 1764 it was extended the four miles from Guildford to Godalming; 32 years later it was joined to the Basingstoke Canal; and in a further 20 years the Wey and Arun Junction Canal was linked to the system, although this latter section was forced to close by the growth of the railway in 1871. William Stevens became the approved wharfinger on the navigation in 1830 and Stevens's barges only ceased to trade commercially on the canal as recently as 1969, six years after Harry Stevens had given the Wey Navigation to the National Trust.

When the Weston family died out Sutton Place went through many changes until the beginning of the 20th century when it was leased by the newspaper baron Lord Northcliffe. Then, in 1917, the Duke of Sutherland took it on. The American oil tycoon Paul Getty put Sutton Place on the tourist trail – Alan Whicker's television interview with the reclusive multi-millionaire is still recalled – but now it is owned by an American trust with visiting strictly controlled.

🍁 TANDRIDGE

At the time of Domesday there was a Tandridge Hundred. Now, more than 900 years later, there is a Tandridge District Council. But the village of Tandridge in the hills near the eastern border with Kent is a quiet little place off the A25. The church, dedicated to St Peter, is well worth visiting because at its western end there is one of Surrey's, if not England's, largest yew trees.

'Though quite hollow it is full of life,' recorded the *Victoria County History*. 'At about 4ft from the ground it spreads out into four great limbs, below which it has a girth of 32 and a half feet. There is a great spread of branches, measuring 81ft from north to south.'

Manning and Bray, those other great Surrey historians, said the lower branches almost caressed the marble tomb of Mrs Scott, wife of the architect Sir George Gilbert Scott. Today, the yew, heavily propped and fortified, does caress the tomb.

Scott, who died at nearby Rooks Nest, which is now a school, designed the north aisle of St Peter's in 1872. The church, which can be traced back to the 12th century, is on the site of pre-Christian worship and it is said that the foundations were built in such a way as not to damage the roots of the already formidable yew.

Tandridge Priory was at the foot of the North Downs and was founded as a hospital, subsequently receiving Augustinian canons. Nothing except the fish ponds remains.

🍁 TATSFIELD

By glancing at a map you can see so easily Tatsfield's position. Surrounded north-west and north-east by Greater London it fits into Surrey like a piece of a jigsaw puzzle. Its lofty heights are very much in the county, though, but look north and you see the London Borough of Bromley in the shape of Biggin Hill which was always in Kent when old-style geography was being taught not too long ago.

Tatsfield vies with Hindhead and Coldharbour for the title of the highest village in Surrey, and it is said that its inhabitants in 1666 saw London burning. Its comparative remoteness even in modern times has led to food parcels having to be dropped by aeroplane when heavy snow blocked the roads.

The 12th century church, whose dedication was not recorded, is 790ft above sea level. There is, as usual in these parts, a very old yew in the churchyard and a tombstone, to one Timothy Burgess who died in 1870, with the following doggerel:

'Once I stood as you do now,
And gaz'd o'er them as you do me;
And you will lie as I do now,
While others thus look down on thee.'

❧ THORPE

'The village is picturesque and consists of a group of houses at the crossroads with others scattered along a winding road to the east.' That was the view of a writer in the first decade of the 20th century, and it holds good today. Of course, there have been vast changes, like the arrival of the aeroplane at Heathrow, the construction of the M3 and M25 motorways, and the development of old gravel pits into a huge water and leisure park.

Thorpe appears to have survived these assaults on its privacy, and the stretch of Coldharbour Lane between the Red Lion and the village hall can be peacefully rural. The pub has been around at least since the start of the 18th century; the village hall for probably a hundred years longer. The latter, which has oak timbers, was a barn in the days when Thorpe was a farming community.

The village was mentioned in the Domesday Book as being held by Chertsey Abbey, but neither St Mary's church nor the mill on the tiny river Bourne was then in existence. St Mary's, which probably dates from the 1300s, stands attractively at the back of a small square off Coldharbour Lane. A 19th century worshipper was Captain Hardy of Nelson fame who had a home in the village.

Great Fosters, a hotel close to Thorpe, has had a chequered history. It is reputed to have been built on the site of one of Henry VIII's hunting lodges and takes its name from Sir Robert Foster, Lord Chief Justice after the Restoration and staunch royalist. Roundhead soldiers made frequent searches of the house during the Civil War when Sir Robert was away with Charles I. And in the 18th century there were again searches when Sir Charles Orbey was the owner, as he was a suspected Jacobite.

In the reign of Good Queen Bess William Marten, a labourer, of Thorpe, was hanged after a jury at Guildford Sessions found him guilty of stealing seven sheep worth 12s. And Thomas Holloway of Egham also went to the gallows when he confessed to the burglary of John Hoult's house at Thorpe and stealing several pieces of linen, a cloak, a hat and a pair of stockings, together valued at £1 16s 4d.

🍁 THURSLEY

This heathy village on the northern slopes of Hindhead is fighting hard to survive. While it may be no bad thing to be bypassed by the busy London to Portsmouth road, only one of its three pubs remains and other services have diminished or disappeared.

But in days long ago Thursley was an important village. It was a staging post on the coach route between the capital and

THE SURREY VILLAGE BOOK ■ THURSLEY

the coast before the long haul over the desolate summit of Hindhead, and was a centre of the Surrey iron industry.

Visitors are attracted by the peace and beauty of the countryside; Thursley Bog is nationally known as a site of special scientific interest.

The churchyard has a stone which marks the grave of a man who was murdered more than 200 years ago. It represents the single most sought out event in the history of the village. The grave to the north of the 950-year-old St Michael and All Angels church tells the story of a foul deed on Hindhead in September 1786. The parish records state: 'September 27, 1786, was buried by the coroner's inquest a man unknown who was murdered on Hindhead on Sunday the 24th of September 1786 by Edward Lonegon, Michael Casey and James Marshall, three sailors who were afterwards hung in chains on Hindhead the 7th of April 1787.'

The unknown man in fact may have been a rich merchant named Hardman who had a love of the sea. A letter in a local newspaper in the 1930s, purporting to have been written by a descendant of the victim, claimed that his wealth had still not been claimed. He was certainly unknown to his three attackers who befriended him on the Portsmouth road and shared his hospitality at the Red Lion at Thursley. But the trio, seeing their 'friend' was a man of means, hatched a plot which unfolded near the 895ft summit of Hindhead. There they murdered the unsuspecting traveller and threw his naked body over the rim of the Devil's Punch Bowl. A shepherd and his boy, who were also in the Red Lion, came across the awful sight as they made their way over Hindhead, and the alarm was raised. The three killers were apprehended further down the Portsmouth road as they tried to sell the dead man's clothes, and were taken to the gaol at Guildford. Once tried and executed, their bodies were returned to Hindhead and hung in chains on the hill then known as Butterwedge.

The bodies, and subsequently skeletons, swung there on that breezy summit for more than three years before they crashed to the ground during a violent thunderstorm. The place became known as Gibbet Hill and is today marked by a granite cross.

A fascination with murder has ensured that the crime is never forgotten. Mysteriously, flowers have appeared on the grave at Thursley on the anniversary of the murder, and, it is claimed, men have died after moving a stone which reminds passers-by of the crime. The original memorial was replaced with one that, on its reverse, contained a warning that it should not be moved. But when the present road was cut in 1826 and subsequently widened the stone was twice moved. Within a year of the last move, in the early 1930s, one of the men involved in the work was dead at the age of 50. Another survived until very old age and, when asked why he thought he had escaped the curse, replied: 'Because I was the driver of the truck and didn't get out of the cab or touch the stone.'

Gibbet Hill and the Devil's Punch Bowl are traditionally linked to Hindhead although they are in the parish of Thursley. The Punch Bowl is a deep hollow which can reflect the mood of the climate, and never more dramatically than on a damp day when mist spills over its rim as if the devil is boiling his cauldron. A few people continue to live in the Punch Bowl but the days when charcoal burners working for the iron industry and broom-makers lived and worked side by side are gone. However, many of the old family names remain in the district and people are proud of their Punch Bowl roots.

Hammer ponds just off the A3 are a reminder of the iron industry. The furnace and forges were usually located in thick woods on quite small streams which were dammed to form the ponds. The water which was accumulated was diverted through an artificial channel to turn a wheel before rejoining the stream lower down.

🍁 TILFORD

This is one of a small number of villages in the county where cricket is played on the green. And it has been that way for more than 110 years. The green is the focal point of Tilford and dotted around its perfect triangular shape are the church, school, institute and pub. Along two of its boundaries runs a river: the Till (more commonly known as the south branch of the Wey) flows in from the west to join the north branch of the Wey in a meadow behind the Barley Mow, and then runs on to Elstead beneath sand cliffs known locally as the Rockies.

Tilford became a village with the building in 1867 of All Saints' church. Until then it was a tithing of Farnham and sometimes called Tilford (or Tylford) Bridge or Tilford Green. The green, as waste of the Manor of Farnham, was handed over to the inhabitants for recreational use in 1835, but the cricket club was not formed until 1886 in spite of the earlier presence of the legendary player, William Beldham, who lived in a cottage on the edge of the green.

'Silver Billy' Beldham came to Tilford when he retired from playing cricket in 1822. He was then aged 55 and had played for Hambledon and on all three London grounds made by Thomas Lord. He was for a time the landlord of the Barley Mow, which has been a pub for the best part of 200 years, but soon moved into Oak Cottage under the spread of Tilford's famous oak tree which Cobbett, in 1822, said was by far the finest he had ever seen.

Alas, the tree is a sorry sight today, but it still stands and must be allowed to do so until it falls naturally. It has been there since the middle of the 17th century. Sadly, one of the three oaks on the green was lost in the Great Storm of October 1987, but has been replaced by a sapling grown from one of its acorns, and is flourishing.

In Beldham's day the old tree was as Cobbett saw it, and it was a popular meeting place. It was sometimes known as Novel's Oak after the name of a local resident. If it could speak what stories it would tell, including the one about how it was rescued from the woodman's axe by local people driving in nails to defy the Bishop of Winchester's instructions. The Bishop, as Lord of the Manor, wanted the oak felled but had not reckoned with the people of Tilford.

Beldham, who was said to be the finest player of his age, lived to be 96. In the census of 1861, when he was in the last year of his life, he listed himself as 'old cricketer'. His home for 40 years still stands but with upstairs accommodation which was added in 1870, soon after the death of his second wife, Ann. The memory of Beldham lives on in the village, and especially in the Barley Mow where it is said his ghost has appeared.

One of my favourite Tilford stories concerns the ice house close to Tilford House. When properly used, it kept meat and fish fresh with the aid of blocks of ice cut from nearby Stockbridge Pond, but it also served as a cooler to sober up the village drunks. The bobby, rather than walk them the three miles into Farnham, simply shut them in the darkened ice house for the night.

Waverley Abbey ruins are close by, and Tilford's bridges were made by the monks. The lines of the west crossing have been hidden by a wartime bridge, erected as a temporary measure and still in use, while the east bridge has been rebuilt.

🍁 TITSEY

To the north of Limpsfield, and separated by the M25 motorway, is Titsey Park, a heavily wooded area which was once the home of the Gresham family. Sir John Gresham pulled down the manor house in 1775 and rebuilt on the same site, and also removed the church of St James, which was a little matter of 35ft from the house, eventually to be rebuilt on its present site on the other side of the road. When the Greshams died out, the park was left to the Leveson-Gower family through marriage, and one of their number was responsible for discovering a Roman villa in the grounds in 1864.

Two Titsey labourers were hanged for breaking into the house of William Gresham in February 1575 and stealing £180. William Morley and Christopher Peryn were sentenced at Croydon Assizes 17 days after they committed the crime. Two yeomen from Titsey had gone to the gallows in the previous year for highway robbery. William Hankyn and Edward Rogers had been found guilty at Southwark Assizes of assaulting Richard Terrye in the highway at Godstone and stealing a cloak and dagger, together valued at 13s, and 2s in money.

🍁 TONGHAM

The village suffers from being in Aldershot's back pocket, and the industrial nature of the Hampshire town tends to rub off on its small neighbour. Also, the Blackwater Valley Road, which links the A31 Hog's Back with the M3, has carved a swathe through its western edge. But for all that there are some pleasant corners in Tongham. On one side of the crossroads is the White Hart, a 600-year-old building. Opposite is an oast house once used for brewing. Now, the Hog's Back Brewery, just up the slope towards the ridge of the North Downs, has returned that quintessential English industry to the village.

Eric Parker wrote in 1908 that the entrance to Tongham from the Hog's Back was by way of 'The Avenue' which was 'pillared and canopied with lofty elms'. The road is now called 'The Street' and the trees disappeared long before elms were felled by the Dutch disease.

Tongham was on the old Farnham to Guildford railway line and passengers used the station until 1937; goods up to 1960, the year before the line closed. In the Great War a building near the station was used as a munitions factory, and in 1939 it became billets for the RASC before being taken over by Tongham Ordnance Depot and being severely damaged by a big explosion and fire at an inflammable store.

The church is dedicated to St Paul and was consecrated in 1866. A son of the first vicar became an Archbishop of York, and at the vicarage there is a plaque which declares that Cyril Forster Garbett was Primate of England from 1947 to 1955.

🍁 VIRGINIA WATER

The lakes and woodland walks to the west of the A30 are crowded at weekends. At times there are probably enough people around to reconstruct the Battle of Culloden. Culloden? Yes, Culloden, the famous Scottish plain east of Inverness where Bonnie Prince Charlie was routed in 1746. The English victor was the Duke of Cumberland who afterwards became Ranger of Windsor Park.

The Duke's deputy was Thomas Sandby, an outstanding architect and landscape gardener, and between them they devised a scheme to drain a large area of marshy ground in the park. Sandby, with the assistance of his brother, Paul, settled on the idea of a vast lake, and today's visitors can thank these 18th century men for their expertise. The lake was enlarged to its present area of around 120 acres later in that century. George IV had a scaled down frigate built for the lake. It was still in use in Queen Victoria's reign and was brought out at her request. A lieutenant and six sailors sailed it along the lake and fired a royal salute from its cannon.

It is perhaps ironic that the victor of Culloden (who was after-

Columns from Leptis Magna, Virginia Water.

wards known as 'Butcher' Cumberland) should have created such beautiful landscape so close to the possible site of even greater butchery in AD 60 – that of the final battle between the Roman 14th Legion and Queen Boudicca's army of Britons in rebellion. There are sound reasons for believing the site to have been between Callow Hill and Knowl Hill – certainly it fulfils the description by Tacitus of the Roman position being approached by a narrow defile with a wood behind and a plain in front.

A little to the west are the genuine remains of a fine Roman building recovered from Leptis Magna near Tripoli in North Africa. They were brought to England and presented to the

Prince Regent in 1816. A proposal to use them for the portico of the British Museum never materialised and they were set up here as a landscape ornament in 1826.

The village of Virginia Water, which has a station, appears to be little more than a dormitory for London. There are many large houses, and the world famous Wentworth Golf Club has attracted millionaire neighbours.

Surrey runs into Berkshire about here – indeed much of the woodland area about the lake is in the Royal County – but the A30 continues to run through Surrey on its way towards the capital, and there are more public gardens and walks before Egham and the Thames are reached.

🍁 WALLISWOOD

A seat beside the former village pump has a plaque that records the fact that Oakwood Village School operated from 1873 to 1994. Its demise came about because of falling numbers of pupils in a rural area, many of whose wealthier residents prefer to send their children to private schools. However, in its place has risen a vibrant nursery school but, of course, these children will not have a truly local first school to attend in time, and will require transport to take them through narrow country lanes to their place of learning. This is a routine acted out daily throughout the county, whose rural transport infrastructure was not designed to cope with school buses and the ubiquitous four-wheel drive vehicles which so many of today's country dwellers seem to believe they need to possess.

Apart from the nursery school and the wonderfully rustic Scarlett Arms public house, Walliswood is no more than a scattered collection of farms and houses. Gatton Manor Golf and Country Club is close by, and so too is Ellen's Green, again no more than a few houses, a pub, the Wheatsheaf and a village hall.

🍁 WALTON-ON-THE-HILL

Walton-on-the-Hill was in the spotlight in 1981 when the Ryder Cup golf tournament was held at Walton Heath. Few of the visitors to that event would have given a second thought to St Peter's church in which there is an 800-year-old lead font, the only one in Surrey and one of only 30 in England. It has a frieze of foliage around its top and its bottom, and there are eight figures, seated, in relief under arches. Not far away, 13th century Walton Place, which lays claim to being the oldest house in the county, was once home to Anne of Cleves.

Lutyens and Jekyll were here in the early part of the 20th century, and much earlier the Romans left their mark. A Romano-British villa at Sandilands Road was excavated in 1948 and contained 13 rooms. It was built in the first century AD, and after being unused for 50 years was renovated and remained in use until around the year AD 400 when it was destroyed.

🍁 WANBOROUGH

It seems improbable now that a tiny collection of buildings just north of the Hog's Back was often, in the late 19th century, the centre of government. When William Ewart Gladstone was Prime Minister, his parliamentary private secretary, Sir Algernon West, was the tenant of Wanborough Manor, and the Liberal leader was a frequent visitor. Cabinet meetings were held there. Queen Victoria also came to stay as the guest of Sir Algernon. Gladstone, in fact, wrote his farewell speech at Wanborough. Herbert Asquith, Liberal Prime Minister from 1908–16, became a sub-tenant of the manor at the beginning of the 20th century, and two of his daughters are buried in the churchyard of St Bartholomew's next door.

The church is the second smallest in the county – it measures 45ft by 18ft, only St Agatha's at Woldingham is smaller – and is 13th century on the site of a Domesday building. When it fell into disrepair in the 1600s it became a carpenter's shop, but as restoration work to Puttenham church, on the other side of the Hog's Back, became necessary, St Bartholomew's was itself restored and reopened in June 1861.

Wanborough was an important farm in the days of Waverley Abbey. About 800 acres were bought in 1130 from a nephew of Queen Adeliza, the second wife of Henry I, and the abbots had a large fish pond just north of the grange. When the abbey was dissolved in 1536 one of the monks, John Parker, went as curate at Wanborough.

A prominent Quaker, Morris Birkbeck, was the tenant of Wanborough Manor at the beginning of the 19th century, before leaving to start a new life in the United States. He founded a community in Illinois, which he called Wanborough, and then, through pamphlets which he wrote, he encouraged many of the agricultural labourers who had worked for him to follow him. Two were the brothers Edward and James Collyer from Elstead, who sailed from Liverpool on the *Achilles* in April 1818 and landed in Philadelphia a month later on 25 May. They made their way overland by wagon, horseback and on foot, and eventually arrived in Wanborough, Illinois, where Birkbeck had built log cabins for them. Two more Collyer brothers, John and William, followed in 1822. Edward met his wife Jane on board the *Achilles* and they married when they had settled in the United States. They had 12 children and some of their descendants still farm the prairies, while others are spread throughout America.

West, the PPS to Gladstone, was a director of the London and South Eastern Railway, and was responsible for having a station sited close to Wanborough so that his important guests might arrive by train. The station is in fact on the edge of Normandy village and was opened in September 1891. The line, which links Reading and Tonbridge via Guildford, was opened in 1847. Nearby is the curiously named Christmas Pie hamlet whose name has been a puzzle for generations. A Christmas Farm is listed on 17th century maps, and a correspondent to the *Surrey Advertiser* in the 1950s stated there was at one time a Pie Farm. Another story runs that there was a farmer named Christmas – a common enough West Surrey name – who had a large family but nothing to eat at the festive season. He went into the woods and bagged some rabbits which his wife cooked into a pie, and the name was coined.

🍁 WARLINGHAM

A gardener was digging his plot one spring day in 1909 when his spade unearthed some pieces of pottery. Further, careful digging uncovered many more fragments and some burnt bones. The site was about 200ft north of the Westerham road between the village and the Hare and Hounds pub and caused much excitement.

An expert was called in and built up the outline of a cinerary urn 10in in diameter, and dated it to the first century. The bones were thought to be that of a child and burnt, presumably, in the urn.

Warlingham has the Greater London boundary to its north and is very much commuter country with a station close by. Here, a century and more ago, young boys whipped the apple trees in spring in an attempt to make them bear more fruit.

All Saints' church is restored 13th century and is reputed to be where the Edward VI-authorised prayer book was first used, when Archbishop Cranmer attended a service. There are some picturesque listed buildings near the green, including the White Lion, which is 18th century, and the almshouses and the vicarage which were both built in 1663.

🍁 WAVERLEY

There never has been a village at Waverley but this area near Farnham has contributed to the beauty of many places in the county. The first Cistercian abbey in England was built here beside the river Wey in 1128 and when it was dissolved in 1536 its stones were used for buildings far and wide. Many of the bridges in the district were undoubtedly built by Waverley monks. The abbey ruins can be seen from the Farnham to Godalming road, and are open to the public.

The road twists violently at Waverley as it crosses the river at the spot where there was a mill, whose miller in the 1570s, Barnard Rowe, was sentenced to hang for theft. He appeared at Croydon Sessions in January 1576 charged with stealing silver, gilt hooks, silver pins, a harness girdle, a silver buckle, five pieces of gold, a sheet, two handkerchiefs and a cassock, together valued at £5 4s 8d, from a widow of Aldershot, Catherine Lague. Rowe's two accomplices, Richard Fowkes, a miller, and Hugh Tarrant, a husbandman, also of Waverley, were 'at large' when he went to the gallows.

Just across the road from the mill site is Stella Cottage, named after Esther Johnson, beloved of Jonathan Swift, whom he called Stella. Swift came to the area as secretary to Sir William Temple, a noted diplomat, who lived in nearby Moor Park, a mansion still standing, which was built in 1630. Swift wrote *Tale of a Tub* there, and undoubtedly meditated in the area around Mother Ludlam's Cave.

The legend of Mother Ludlam, the white witch of Waverley, has been handed down to children through the ages. Her cave is tatty now, tattier no doubt than when Cobbett wrote in 1825: 'Alas it is no longer the enchanting place that I knew it. The semi-circular palings are gone; the basins to catch the never-ceasing little streams are gone, the iron cups, fastened by chains for people to drink out of, are gone; the pavement all broken to pieces; the seats for people to sit on, on both sides of the cave, torn up and gone; the stream that ran down through a clean paved channel, now making a dirty gutter; and the ground opposite, which was a grove chiefly of laurels, inter-sected by closely mown grass walks, now become a poor ragged-looking alder coppice.'

🍁 WESTCOTT

The man who gave us the *Principle of Population* was born in Westcott. Thomas Malthus, a clergyman and economist, con-tended that as population increased faster than the means of subsistence, its growth could only be checked by normal restraint or by disease and war. Malthus (1766-1832) was born at The Rookery to the south of Coast Hill on the west side of the village. His father, David, bought the house with its extensive grounds which he landscaped by using the Pippbrook stream to the full.

There was a mill at The Rookery and another at Westcott. In fact, the tiny Pippbrook, which rises on the northern slopes of Leith Hill and flows for only a matter of a few miles to join the Mole, at one time supplied the water for six mills. Westcott became an ecclesiastical parish, separate from Dorking, in 1852 when the Sir George Gilbert Scott-designed Holy Trinity church opened. The church and burial ground occupy a fine site above the A25 and are approached through a lych gate which was provided by public subscription in 1890. The village is attractive in spite of the rush of traffic, with a green on which there is a dovecote. Nearby is a public house whose name is again The Cricketers after a short period as, of all things, The Wizard.

South of the village, in Squire's Wood, there was in times past a watering hole by the name of Mag's Well. It was said to be a medicinal spring and children bathed in it.

🍁 WEST END

General Charles Gordon of Khartoum is remembered here by the Gordon School, founded originally as the Gordon Boys' Home at a cost of £24,000 in 1885. Gordon had been killed when a siege on the British garrison in the Sudanese capital succeeded on 26 January in that year. He and his under-strength staff had held out for ten months. Two days later the expeditionary force belatedly sent out by Gladstone arrived in Khartoum. Gordon had gone to Sudan to establish a government when Gladstone had ordered the Egyptians out of that

9

The statue of General Gordon that stands in the school grounds at West End.

country. But having evacuated thousands of women and children, the Sudanese religious leader, who had earlier routed the Anglo-Egyptian forces, surrounded the city and Gordon was trapped. Almost a century later, many of Gordon's effects were sold at auction in Farnham, having been stored prior to the sale in a large house, long since demolished, close to the town centre.

❧ WESTHUMBLE

Down on the valley floor in Westhumble a chapel was built because of the difficulty in getting across the Mole to the nearest parish church. In an early 19th century publication, *The Promenade round Dorking*, it is recorded that the Mole had rapid currents and such depth that a boat was upset and several gentlemen drowned. The river dries up and goes underground in very hot spells which gives credence to the claim of Celia Fiennes that 'just about Dorken and Leatherhead it sinkes away in many places which they call swallow holes'.

At Westhumble is the Burford Bridge Hotel where, when it was known as the Fox and Hounds, Nelson spent his last night ashore before the Battle of Trafalgar, and farewelled Lady Hamilton.

Since the 1980s, Denbies vineyard on the southern chalk slopes of Ranmore has become the leading producer of wine in the country, and a major tourist attraction.

❧ WEYBOURNE

A ribbon development village between Farnham and Aldershot. John Henry Knight, the inventor and motoring pioneer, was born at Weybourne House in 1847 and moved to

Barfield at nearby Runfold in 1888. Knight was a man clearly ahead of his time, whether it be in the motoring field or in photography, and there is a fascinating collection of examples of his work in the district which periodically surfaces. His birthplace was believed to have been built in 1729 by Peter Coldham who was at one time the owner of Waverley Abbey near Farnham. Farnham Council purchased the property in 1947.

Weybourne's two pubs are old established hostelries. The Elm Tree stands near the crossroads and presumably takes its name from a large elm tree that stood proudly by the roadside. The Running Stream is very close to the Hampshire border and was the local of a well-known Farnham character who was known to all as the rag and bone man. His horse and cart were daily to be seen outside the Running Stream; indeed it was suggested, probably unfairly, that it was the only pub in the district which extended the man a welcome.

🍁 WHITELEY VILLAGE

When William Whiteley came south from his native Yorkshire in 1851 he could not have realised what effect that would have in the 20th century. Whiteley, who died in 1907, left one million pounds which was to be used to build a retirement village, and today that community thrives.

Whiteley was born in 1831 and when he was 20 he journeyed down to London to view the Great Exhibition. He liked the capital enough to want to stay and ten years later opened a small shop in Westbourne Grove. That business grew into Whiteley's Store in Bayswater and made William Whiteley a millionaire.

The person to whom Whiteley had taken his idea, the Bishop of London, Dr Winnington-Ingram, became the first

WINDLESHAM ▣ *THE SURREY VILLAGE BOOK*

chairman of the trustees, and was joined by the philan-
thropist's two sons. Whiteley stipulated that the village was to
be west of London, no more than ten miles from Charing
Cross, and not to be sited on clay soil. They were instructions
that could not be met mainly because of the nature of the land
around the capital, and eventually a site was settled on 17
miles out on the Burhill Estate of Viscount Iveagh. It was land
where pines and rhododendrons grew in profusion and the soil
was typically Surrey: sandy.

Six architects were invited to submit designs and Robert
Frank Atkinson was commissioned to proceed with his vision
of an octagonal community with a memorial to Whiteley as
the centrepiece. Five other architects then joined Atkinson in
designing the buildings. Work started shortly before the Great
War and by Armistice Day a few people had moved in.

The church of St Mark was dedicated by the Bishop of
Winchester on the saint's day, 25 April, in 1918, and by the
time King George V and Queen Mary visited the village in
1920 to open the social centre, 284 people were in residence.

Whiteley Village today nestles in the comfortable and well-
heeled hinterland of Weybridge and Esher, and is thought to
be a unique idea in community living.

🍁 WINDLESHAM

Aubrey enthused over this place on the western edge of
Chobham Common when he was on his walkabout through
the county. He fastened on to the reputation for growing bog-
myrtle, and wrote: 'In this parish, at Light-Water-Moor, grows
great store of a plant, about a foot and a half high, called by
the inhabitants Gole, but the true name is Gale; it has a very
grateful smell, like a mixture of bays and myrtle, and in Latin
is called Myrtus Brabantica; it grows also in several places of

this healthy country, and is used to be put in their chests among their linnen.'

The church of St John the Baptist went up in 1680 four years after its predecessor had been struck by lightning. In the churchyard there is a gravestone with the curious epitaph:

'She was, but words are wanting to say "What",
Thinking what a wife should be, and she was "That".'

The men from Windlesham who were killed in the Great War are remembered by a Celtic cross which was unveiled by Hermione, Lady Ellenborough of Windlesham Court in 1920. They would have remembered the village as it was described by Eric Parker: '...straggles over a dozen short crooked roads – an oasis among parallelograms.'

🍁 WISLEY

Wisley means the Royal Horticultural Society gardens, which are visited by tens of thousands of people every year. The gardens came into the possession of the RHS following the death of the society's treasurer, George Ferguson Wilson, a scientist and inventor who had bought 60 acres of land at Wisley in 1878 and developed an experimental garden. They were purchased by Sir Thomas Hanbury, a Quaker, who gave them to the RHS in 1903. The following year the society moved from its garden at Chiswick, which it had leased since 1822. The area is four times what it was in Mr Wilson's day when Eric Parker wrote that 'experiment and officialdom have settled heavily on its sandy soil, and the wilder charm of the old pleasance has left it'. Parker observed that in Mr Wilson's day the gardens were a delight to many hundreds of visitors. Wisley has clearly improved with age.

There was uproar in 1869 when the locals got to hear of a proposal to enclose 362 acres of Wisley Common, and the plan was dropped. Since then, development has eroded much of the countryside but Bolder Mere remains. It is a 10-acre shallow lake, favoured by windsurfers, and previously beloved of customers of the Hut Hotel which stood on the opposite side of the Portsmouth Road. Sadly, that hostelry was demolished in the name of progress, or at least a faster stretch of A3, just as the Half Moon at Thursley disappeared long before that section of the same trunk road was transformed into a dual carriageway.

The village of Wisley is a mile or so from the Gardens and is very rural. The lane which serves as the main street wanders between houses, crosses quite a wide stretch of the Wey and bends past the little Norman church. Beside the church, which has no dedication, is a delightful old farmhouse and the two taken together epitomise the timelessness of the area, notwithstanding that, like so many of Surrey's byways, the lane through Wisley has become a shortcut and a 'rat run' in an attempt to avoid traffic hold-ups elsewhere.

🍁 WITLEY

Traffic races through the village on its way to Sussex and the coast which is no way to see its beauty and its charm. Witley has been a thriving place for a long time. Its church was recorded in the Domesday Book, and the court of Edward I met at the White Hart Inn for four days from 8 June 1305.

The parish once was in four tithings: Milford and Mousehill; Ley or Lea which included Wheeler Street; Stoatley; and Birtley which included Witley Street and Witley Park. The modern parish of Witley encompasses the villages of Milford, Wormley and Brook and district. A railway station means the area is home for commuters who can enjoy fast travel to London while living among beautiful undulating South West Surrey pineland.

Social troubles in 1549 led to riots in Witley. The 'general rebellion' in these parts was largely against the enclosing of lands. One of those who rebelled may have been John Porter, a farmer, of Witley. Some 23 years later he strangled his wife Margery as she lay asleep, and a jury at Southwark Assizes on 26 February 1573 found him guilty and he was sentenced to death by hanging.

At the top of Church Lane in the early part of the 19th century there was a semaphore station for relaying messages between the Admiralty in London and ships off Portsmouth. The stations either side of Bannicle, as Witley's was known, were at Pewley in Guildford and Haste Hill at Haslemere. Families of the men worshipped at All Saints' church which with its attendant group of cottages comprises one of the most pleasant corners in the county. Step Cottage, close to the church, has been photographed so often it must be known around the world.

All Saints is one of seven churches in the county which contains Saxon work. In 1889, a three-tiered 12th century fresco representing scenes from the life of Christ was uncovered, having been limewashed over during the Reformation, and more than 100 years later another great work of art, The *Harrowing of Hell*, was also revealed.

🍁 WOLDINGHAM

In the 1970s a plan by the Government to build a rail link to the then much talked about Channel Tunnel raised the hackles of local people. The plan was to use land at Marden Park for the terminus, but the public outcry was such that the idea was abandoned. Back in 1836 there was a similar outpouring of concern over plans to drive the railway through the area. The pre-Victorian worthies won that day and their successors wrangled for almost 50 years before losing out as the railway network took a hold. The Croydon and East Grinstead line opened in 1884 and a long tunnel took it under Woldingham. A garden village was built near the station during the First World War, and first saw life as an army camp.

St Agatha's church, first mentioned in 1270, is the smallest in the county at 30ft 3in by 20ft 2in. And at 797ft above sea level it is the third highest old parish church in Surrey, behind those at Coldharbour and Abinger. The village's other church, St Paul's, was built in 1905.

🍁 WONERSH

Wonersh Blue was famous in Elizabethan times. No, it wasn't cheese but cloth. This was a cloth-making centre and the clothiers dyed their garments with woad. The trade in blue cloth from Wonersh was particularly brisk in the Canary Islands, but eventually greed got the better of the manufacturers whose dishonesty in stretching their webs was their downfall. By the 17th century cloth-making had dwindled to next to nothing in the district.

The pub in the centre of the village is called the Grantley Arms after the family who owned the big house in Wonersh Park. Sir Fletcher Norton, who became the first Baron

Grantley, was the Speaker of the House of Commons from 1769 to 1782. His grandson, George, had an unhappy marriage and kidnapped his children, holding them hostage at Wonersh Park. His wife Caroline's fight to get them back eventually led to the Custody of Infants Bill becoming law in 1839.

The mansion was demolished in the 1930s and some land that had been enclosed was returned to the people as a village green. The 11th-century church of St John the Baptist is close by and was rebuilt in 1796 to, according to one legend, the design of Lord Grantley's butler after fire had greatly damaged it three years earlier. The church, which once had fine box pews and a triple decker pulpit, was restored at the beginning of the 20th century.

It was the centre of attention in 1989 when the then vicar, the Rev Tom Farrell, a top British athlete in his younger days, wanted to remove a carved rood screen to allow his evangelical-style ministry to flourish. Mr Farrell incurred the wrath of more than 460 villagers and this led to a three-day Consistory Court being held before a judge who eventually found in favour of the vicar. Among those who gave evidence was an elderly resident who remembered when the screen was installed. She said: 'There was a lot of opposition to the screen, but we were a much smaller community then. It is interesting that there was the same proportion of people against the screen as now want to keep it.'

The imposing red-bricked building of St John's Seminary, which celebrated its centenary in 1991, dominates the southern entrance to the village. It is one of only four seminaries in Britain, and life for the trainee priests changed as a result of the Second Vatican Council in 1967. Then, a greater emphasis began to be placed on personal responsibility rather than the previous detailed rules which dictated daily life. At the centenary celebrations, this change prompted the rector, who had trained at St John's a quarter of a century earlier, to observe that in his day he had not even been allowed a newspaper; now students were allowed both radio and television.

🍁 WOODMANSTERNE

The greatest horse race in the world has its origins in this com-muter village close to the Greater London boundary. In 1780 the horse-racing enthusiast twelfth Earl of Derby was living at The Oaks and he founded the Epsom Downs classic, and also lent the name of his home to its companion event. Today, The Derby and The Oaks are part of a great carnival of racing at Epsom at the beginning of June. Classics of another kind were also connected with Woodmansterne: the artist John Constable and the author Charles Dickens often stayed with friends who lived in the village.

🍁 WOOD STREET VILLAGE

North-west of Guildford and part of the parish of Worplesdon. Residents were right to request the word 'Village' be added to their address, because Wood Street on its own gives quite the wrong impression. Broadstreet Common, which runs around the south-western edge, gives the village a rural feel, and the green and its neighbouring pub attract many visitors. It is the first open space north of the Guildford to Reading railway line after leaving the county town, and long may it continue to be so.

🍁 WORMLEY

This scattered area between Witley and Chiddingfold has at its heart King Edward's School which commands attention on the crest of the hill on the main road. The school came to Surrey in 1867 to cater for destitute boys who, recorded the *Victoria County History*, 'have never been committed of crime and who are trained for the army, navy or industrial life'. It had been founded in London in 1552. Today, King Edward's takes girls as well and has an outstanding academic and sporting name, as befits an establishment which had an Olympic Games representative, the Rev A.C.B. Bellerby, as headmaster from 1926 to 1961. During the war Mr Bellerby, his staff and pupils were installed in the Institute at nearby Hambledon while King Edward's was taken over by the Admiralty which developed naval radar there – almost a century and a half after the Admiralty relied on a semaphore station at Bannicle in neighbouring Witley to get its messages to the ships off Spithead.

The wartime radar work at King Edward's was used in the Battle of the Atlantic, and Wormley continued to have a link with the sea through the presence of the Institute of Oceanographic Science, whose headquarters were situated close to the school until recently.

🍁 WORPLESDON

In the days of the semaphore system of sending messages via the Admiralty in London and the ships in the Channel, Worplesdon was one of the stations on the ill-fated line to Plymouth. The semaphore building was a tower adjacent to the church and a contemporary print displays a peaceful scene with sheep grazing outside the churchyard wall. Worplesdon

Glebe Station was demolished in 1851, two decades after the line was abandoned. The branch to Plymouth had begun in 1825 from Chatley Heath on Ockham Common, where there was a station on the line to Portsmouth. Worplesdon and Poyle Hill (Hog's Back) were the Surrey stations before the messages entered Hampshire.

St Mary's church was described at the turn of the century as being on the 'summit of a gentle hill in a churchyard of considerable beauty'. Even in the built-up nineties, the area of the church retains that quality. Worplesdon is a parish of contrasts and far enough removed from Guildford to have a peaceful air about it.

Whitmoor Common has been claimed as the place of Wibbandun where Caeulin, King of the West Saxons, met Ethelbert, King of Kent, in battle in AD 568. And at Slyfield Green, which is now part of industrial Guildford, Aubrey recorded that there had been an attempt to find coal. The would-be miner was the Rev Giles Thornborough, rector of St Nicolas and Trinity, Guildford, who in 1671 found a type of stony coal when grubbing the roots of an old oak tree. Aubrey wrote that Thornborough dug to a depth of about 150ft and found a rocky coal but after £400 had been spent the pit fell in.

A Worplesdon man who was more successful was Benjamin Martin who began life as a plough boy and ended it as an optician in Fleet Street where he died in 1782, aged 77. Martin learned the three Rs and taught them in Guildford before studying mathematics and astronomy and travelling the country.

❧ WOTTON

This is Evelyn country. The famous diarist, John Evelyn, was born at Wotton House and is buried in the church of St John

Wotton, Surrey

the Evangelist on the other side of the A25. A descendant, Patrick, was the county's high sheriff in 1982. Wotton House came into the Evelyn family in 1579 when John's grandfather, George, bought it.

The church is down a lane and looks out over the North Downs. It is the family burial place of the Evelyns and, said John, was where he received the rudiments of his education. 'I was not initiated into any rudiments till I was four years of age, and then one Frier taught us at the church porch of Wotton.'

A church at Wotton is not mentioned in the Domesday Book although it has been suggested that part of it is early Norman. Wotton Hundred at the time of the survey stretched from Abinger Hammer in the west to Betchworth in the east, and Wotton, which had been held by Harold, was then held by Oswald. There was a mill recorded and this seems certain to have been at Friday Street, a mile or two south and now a favourite haunt of ramblers.

❧ WRECCLESHAM

If there was a title awarded to the best beer-drinking village in Surrey then Wrecclesham, on performances admittedly more past than present, would surely win. As Alice Holt Forest receded, hop-bines were planted and the area outside Farnham became a vast garden for the numerous ale houses and breweries. One hundred or so years ago the situation so disgusted an Australian who had come to live in Farnham that he wrote to a Liberal publication, *The Speaker*, as follows: 'There is one licence to every 126 inhabitants (in Farnham), with the result that during the eight months I have been in the district I have seen more drunk people than during the previous 12 years in Adelaide, with a population more than ten times as large. It is very necessary that something be done to lessen the evil, which is even worse in the surrounding villages. About two miles from here is a village called Wreekelsham (sic), with a population of 600, and in its main street there are five licensed houses within 200 yards, besides another in a side street, and several grocer's licences. On Monday afternoons the whole village is drunk, and one has to drive through it very carefully.' Tut, tut. The local newspaper also published the letter and with one eye on its circulation figures defended its readers. The allegation was a 'statement so foolish as not to be worthy of contradiction'.

There are three pubs now in the main street and one, the Cricketers, recalls the glory it knew back in the late 18th and early 19th centuries when it was 'home' to two of the greatest players of the noble game in Georgian times. William 'Silver Billy' Beldham and 'Honest' John Wells were brothers-in-law and used the Cricketers as their local. Beldham's brother John was at one time the landlord and for many years the hostelry bore the signs: 'Rendezvous of those great cricketers, Beldham and Wells' and 'Village's best beer as drunk by those famous men, Beldham and Wells'. Beldham, the son of a yeoman farmer, was born in 1766 in what is now Old Yew Tree Cottage in Wrecclesham. He joined the famous Hambledon club in 1787 and was a giant of the game for 40 years. A hoax played on the 19th century cricket historian and statistician, Arthur Haygarth, led to the myth that Beldham fathered 39 children, but extensive research by this author has established that from two marriages (his first wife died soon after giving birth to her first child) he was the father of nine, and from the line through the son he named William there are descendants living in Dorset and Kent who came together in 1982 when Beldham was remembered as a founder of Farnham Cricket Club 200 years earlier.

Because of the proximity of the forest, Wrecclesham's

inhabitants were often referred to as 'outlaws'. They were said to be a lawless breed. It would have been a wild place at the time of Domesday when its two mills were probably among the six recorded as being in the Farnham Hundred. The mills were not named in the 1086 survey. Wrecclesham's were Willey, now a private house, and Weydon, or Le Medmulle, whose sluices can be detected just off the Farnham bypass.

Willey stands beside the A31 and close to the county boundary. The water meadows on the banks of the Wey contrast nicely with the trees of Alice Holt Forest. This area is known as Runwick and lanes climb northwards into Hampshire. Wrecclesham is well known for its blue gault clay, and the pottery on high ground behind the Royal Oak has been in existence since 1873. It was founded by Absolam Harris, who had worked clay at Charles Hill, Tilford, and was continued by his son William, then grandsons Reg and Arthur, and, until his death in 1983, great grandson Reg. In the 1980s the family said there was a deposit of blue clay at the pottery which could last for 40 years.

Now the pottery has taken on a new direction thanks to the involvement of the Farnham Buildings Preservation Trust which has bought the premises and produced a strategic plan to take one of the longest surviving industries in the county forward into the 21st century.

A notice in the *Surrey Advertiser* of 9 February 1910 reported the death of John Barnett, of Clay Hill Cottages, Wrecclesham, aged 86, who was said to be one of the dwindling band of Indian Mutiny veterans. He accepted the Queen's shilling when he enlisted in the 70th Foot in 1842 at the Swan, an old hostelry in East Street, Farnham, which is where the recruiting sergeant was based, there being no military presence in Aldershot at that time. He went with his regiment to Peshawar at the time of the Indian Mutiny in 1857 and, said the newspaper account, although he took no part in the fighting he had to carry out the unenviable task of assisting in the executions by shooting and hanging thousands of the mutineers. He left the army after 18 years and was able to live his declining years in comfort due to a weekly pension of seven shillings from the War Office and another from Lord Roberts's veterans' fund.

🍁 WYKE

Lord Pirbright, who took his name from the neighbouring village, is buried in the churchyard at Wyke, beside the Guildford to Aldershot road and in the parish of Normandy. He lived at Henley Park, midway between Pirbright and Wyke, and was a generous benefactor to the village whose name he bore. Before taking his title, he was Henry de Worms, son of Solomon de Worms who had come to England in 1815 and married a Rothschild. Henry succeeded William Ewart Gladstone as MP for Greenwich and was the first Jew to become a Privy Councillor.

❧ BIBLIOGRAPHY

Books on Surrey are numerous, but many are out of print and hard to obtain. My collection has been put together through years of ferreting in secondhand shops. Three titles, *History of Surrey* by H.E. Malden, first published in 1900, *Highways and Byways in Surrey* by Eric Parker, written in 1908, and *Surrey* (the Buildings of England series) by Ian Nairn and Nikolaus Pevsner, who died within a few days of one another in 1984, are required reading by any student of the county. Much earlier came the Manning and Bray volumes, Brayley's history, the *Victoria County History* series and Aubrey's writings, which are in main libraries. Many village history societies and local authorities have published material which is available at the new Surrey History Centre in Woking. Much of my material has come from notes collected over the years, and from the files of the *Surrey Advertiser* and the *Farnham Herald* newspapers.

INDEX

Abinger 11
Abinger Hammer 12
Albury 13
Alfold 15
Artington 16
Ash 18
Ashford 19
Ash Green 20
Ash Vale 21

Badshot Lea 21
Bagshot 22
Baynards 32
Beacon HIll 24
Betchworth 25
Birtley Green (see Grafham) 100
Bisley 26
Blackheath 27
Bletchingley 27
Blindley Heath 29
Bookham (Great and Little) 29,
    30
Bourne, The 30
Bowlhead Green 32
Box Hill 33
Bramley 33
Brockham 35
Brook 35
Brookwood 37
Buckland 38
Burpham 39
Burstow 40
Busbridge 41
Byfleet 42

Capel 45
Caterham 45
Catteshall 46
Chaldon 48

Charlwood 49
Chelsham 50
Chiddingfold 50
Chilworth 52
Chipstead 54
Chobham 54
Christmas Pie (see Wanborough)
    199
Churt 56
Clandon (East and West) 58, 59
Claygate 60
Cobham 50
Coldharbour 62
Compton 63
Cox Green 66
Cranleigh 67
Crowhurst 68

Deepcut 69
Dippenhall 69
Ditton, Thames 71
Dockenfield 71
Dormansland 72
Downside 72
Dunsfold 73

Eashing 74
East Clandon 58
East Horsley 117
East Molesey (see Moleseys) 137
Effingham 75
Egham 75
Elstead 77
Englefield Green 80
Esher 81
Ewhurst 82

Fairlands 82
Farleigh 83

Farley Green 84
Farncombe 85
Felbridge 88
Fetcham 88
Forest Green 89
Frensham 91
Friday Street 94
Frimley 94
Frimley Green 95

Gatton 96
Godstone 97
Gomshall 99
Grafham 100
Grayswood 100
Great Bookham 29

Hale 101
Hambledon 104
Hascombe 105
Haxted 108
Headley 109
Heath End 110
Hersham 111
Hinchley Wood 111
Hindhead 112
Holmbury St Mary 114
Holmwood 115
Horne 116
Horsell 116
Horsley (East and West) 118
Hurtmore 119
Hydestile 120

Jacobs Well 122

Kingswood 122
Knaphill 123

Laleham 123
Leigh 124
Lightwater 124
Limpsfield 126

Lingfield 128
Little Bookham 30
Littleton (Guildford) 129
Littleton (Spelthorne) 130
Long Ditton (see Dittons) 71
Lower Bourne (see The Bourne)
    30
Lower Kingswood (see Kingswood)
    122
Lyne 131

Mayford 132
Merrow 133
Merstham 134
Mickleham 134
Middle Bourne (see The Bourne)
    30
Milford 136
Moleseys (East and West) 137
Munstead 138
Mytchett 139

Newchapel 140
Newdigate 140
Normandy 141
Norney 143
North Holmwood (see Holmwood)
    115
Nutfield 144

Oakwoodhill 145
Ockham 146
Ockley 147
Old Woking 149
Onslow Village 149
Ottershaw 150
Outwood 151
Oxshott 152
Oxted 152

Peaslake 153
Peasmarsh 154
Peper Harow 155

Pirbright 156
Pixham 158
Puttenham 158
Pyrford 160

Ripley 161
Rowledge 163
Rowly 164
Runfold 165
Rushmoor 166

Salfords 167
Sandhills 167
Sands, The 168
Seale 169
Send 170
Shackleford 172
Shalford 174
Shamley Green 175
Shepperton 176
Shere 177
Shottermill 180
Smallfield 181
South Holmwood (see Holmwood)
    115
Stanwell 181
Stoke d' Abernon 182
Sunbury 183
Sutton (see Abinger) 11
Sutton Green 184

Tanbridge 185
Tatsfield 186
Thames Ditton (see Ditton,
    Thames) 71
The Bourne 30
The Sands 168

Thorpe 187
Thursley 188
Tilford 191
Titsey 192
Tongham 193

Upper Bourne (see The Bourne)
    30

Virginia Water 194

Walliswood 196
Walton-on-the-Hill 197
Wanborough 197
Warlingham 199
Waverley 200
West Clandon 59
Westcott 201
West End 202
West Horsley 118
Westhumble 204
West Molesey (see Moleseys) 137
Weybourne 204
Whiteley Village 205
Windlesham 206
Wisley 207
Witley 209
Woldingham 210
Wonersh 211
Woodmansterne 213
Wood Street Village 213
Wormley 214
Worplesdon 214
Wotton 215
Wrecclesham 217
Wyke 220